RETAIL MARKETING

RETAIL MARKETING

Dr. S. BANUMATHY,
M.Com., MBA., M.Phil., Ph.D.,
Associate Prof & Head,
Department of Commerce,
V. V. Vanniaperumal College for Women,
Virudhunagar.

Dr. M. JAYALAKSHMI,
M.Com., M.Phil., Ph.D.,
Associate Professor,
Department of Commerce,
S. F. R. College for Women,
Sivakasi.

Himalaya Publishing House

ISO 9001:2008 CERTIFIED

First Edition : 2010
Reprint : 2015
Edition : 2017
Edition : 2018

Published by : Mrs. Meena Pandey for **Himalaya Publishing House Pvt. Ltd.,**
"Ramdoot", Dr. Bhalerao Marg, Girgaon, **Mumbai - 400 004.**
Phone: 022-23860170/23863863, Fax: 022-23877178
E-mail: himpub@vsnl.com; Website: www.himpub.com

Branch Offices

New Delhi : "Pooja Apartments", 4-B, Murari Lal Street, Ansari Road, Darya Ganj, New Delhi - 110 002. Phone: 011-23270392, 23278631; Fax: 011-23256286

Nagpur : Kundanlal Chandak Industrial Estate, Ghat Road, Nagpur - 440 018. Phone: 0712-2738731, 3296733; Telefax: 0712-2721216

Bengaluru : Plot No. 91-33, 2nd Main Road Seshadripuram, Behind Nataraja Theatre, Bengaluru-560020. Phone: 08041138821, 9379847017, 9379847005

Hyderabad : No. 3-4-184, Lingampally, Besides Raghavendra Swamy Matham, Kachiguda, Hyderabad - 500 027. Phone: 040-27560041, 27550139

Chennai : New-20, Old-59, Thirumalai Pillai Road, T. Nagar, Chennai - 600 017. Mobile: 9380460419

Pune : First Floor, "Laksha" Apartment, No. 527, Mehunpura, Shaniwarpeth (Near Prabhat Theatre), Pune - 411 030. Phone: 020-24496323/24496333; Mobile: 09370579333

Lucknow : House No. 731, Shekhupura Colony, Near B.D. Convent School, Aliganj, Lucknow - 226 022. Phone: 0522-4012353; Mobile: 09307501549

Ahmedabad : 114, "SHAIL", 1st Floor, Opp. Madhu Sudan House, C.G. Road, Navrang Pura, Ahmedabad - 380 009. Phone: 079-26560126; Mobile: 09377088847

Ernakulam : 39/176 (New No.: 60/251) 1st Floor, Karikkamuri Road, Ernakulam, Kochi – 682011. Phone: 0484-2378012, 2378016; Mobile: 09387122121

Bhubaneswar : 5 Station Square, Bhubaneswar - 751 001 (Odisha). Phone: 0674-2532129, Mobile: 09338746007

Kolkata : 108/4, Beliaghata Main Road, Near ID Hospital, Opp. SBI Bank, Kolkata - 700 010, Phone: 033-32449649, Mobile: 7439040301

DTP by : Shubhangi S.G.

Printed at : M/S Sri Sai Art Printer Hyderabad. On behalf of HPH.

FOREWORD

I have great pleasure in contributing foreword to the book entitled 'Retail Marketing'. In recent years, Retailing has become one of the important thrust areas of Commerce and Management attracting the attention of academicians.

Retailing comprises of business activities involved in selling goods and services to consumers for personal and family use. Retailing is the last stage in the distribution process. Today, retailing has many challenges ahead. Indian retailers need to adopt themselves to the complex, challenging, competitive environment.

This text book on 'Retail Marketing' provides various insights into the retail business for the readers. The salient features of the Book are:

- Logical presentation, starting with basic issues and then moving on to a detailed explanation about the 6 p's namely product, price, people, presentation, place and promotion, and finally explaining about the overall retailing with case analysis.
- Presentation in simple language so that students can easily grasp.
- Suitable examples from Indian retail sector to simplify the topic.
- Incorporating latest developments.
- Review questions at the end of each chapter for better understanding and quick revision by the students for examination purpose.

The present publication 'Retail Marketing' represents a timely effort to focus attention on the vital issues in retail business. The publication will be a valuable and useful addition to all Commerce and Management libraries.

Dr.V. Alagappan, ***M.Com., Ph.D.***,
Registrar, (i/c)
Madurai Kamaraj University,
Madurai — 625021,
Tamil Nadu.

PREFACE

The success of any business firm or industry is largely determined by its ability in making the products. In recent years, vast changes are happening in the production and distribution of goods throughout the world, especially in the developing countries. In a developing country like India, we see a rise in the purchasing power, growth of middleclass following western lifestyle and change in fashion. Still, large part of the population is concentrated only in rural area. Hence, the Indian retail scenario is very much different from that of the western developed countries. Though organized retailing is slowly growing, our Indian retail market is dominated only by unorganized retailing. Although retailing in its various formats has been operated in our country for a long time, it is only in the form of "Mom and Pop" Stores.

Only in the twenty first–century, an ever–increasing series of changes happened in retailing. Retailers are increasing the sophistication of retail operation and decision making tools for coordinating their supply chains, buying merchandise and managing store operations. At this time, when retailing in India is going through a transformation, there is a compelling need to understand the retail phenomenon systematically. As Indian retail scenario is changing and competing with global giants, explaining the concepts with domestic examples and references is the need of the hour. Hence, this book on retail marketing with references and examples from the Indian retail sector is sure to help the learners for better learning. This book will prove of immense utility to students for their degree and other competitive examinations.

Authors

CONTENTS

Chapter 1

RETAIL MARKETING – AN OVERVIEW

INTRODUCTION

Retailing is one of the oldest business of mankind. As the development of human civilization took place, the direct business transaction from producer to consumer gave way to direct marketing. In the modern business world, any business to consumer world, any business to consumer interaction can be termed as retailing interaction and can be termed as retailing. Retailing is the final stage of any economic activity.

According to Philip Kotler, "Retailing includes all the activities involved in selling goods or services to the final consumers for personal or non-personal use".

A retailer or retail store is any business enterprise whose sales volume comes from retailing. Retailing can be dealt with in different perspectives. Retailer is considered as one of the channel members in distribution. In this case, the retailer is serving as a postman delivering the products/services of the manufacturer. The role of retailer is simply executing the requirements of the marketer. Any organization selling to final consumer is doing retailing. Retailing is the final step in the distribution of merchandise for consumption by the end consumers. Thus, the retailer is the last link to consumer in the channel of distribution from manufacturer to consumer. As the retailer is working close to consumers, they are able to understand the changing taste and preferences of consumers. Retailers' feedback about consumers helps the manufacturers to convert the needs and wants of consumers into a real product in hand. Thus, retailing is the most dynamic business.

Retailing is any firm selling products in small quantities to final consumers for ultimate consumption purpose. It consists of all activities involved in the marketing of goods and services directly to the final consumers for their personal, family or household use. A retailer is a company or an organisation that purchases products from individuals or companies with the intent to resell those goods/services to the final consumers.

Retailing is such a part of our everyday lives that it is often taken for granted. Customers are not aware of the sophisticated business decisions taken by the retail managers. The modern technologies adopted by the retailers are facilitating the consumers to choose their required goods and services among various varieties and brands. Retail managers are making complex decisions in selecting target markets, retail locations, merchandise and service to offer, negotiation with suppliers, motivating sales associates and deciding how to price, promote and present the merchandise in the retail outlet. In the consumer oriented marketing, retailing may be redefined as the first point of consumer contact.

FUNCTIONS OF A RETAILER

From customer point of view, retailers supply the required goods, at affordable price, at the required time, in the required place. Thus, retailer creates time, place and possession utilities. Besides that, in modern retailing, it is the retailer who performs numerous functions for satisfying the needs of the ultimate consumers. Retailer perform various functions like sorting, breaking bulk, holding stock, as a channel of communication, advertising, storage and certain additional services, which are as follows:

1. Sorting: Manufacturer usually make one or a variety of products and would like to sell their entire inventory to a few buyers to reduce costs. Final consumer, in contrast prefer a large variety of goods and services to choose from and usually buy them in small quantities. Retailers are able to balance the demands of both sides, by collecting an assortment of goods from different sources, buy them in sufficiently large quantities, and sell them to consumers in small units. This process is referred to as the sorting process. Through this process, retailers undertake activities and perform functions that add to the value of the products and services sold to the consumer. Supermarkets offer, on an average, 15,000 different items from 500 companies. Consumers are able to choose from a wide range of designs, sizes, and brands from just one location. If each manufacturer had a separate store for its own products, consumers would have to visit several stores to complete their shopping. While all retailers offer an assortment, they specialize in certain types of assortment offered and the market to which the offering is made. For example, Westside provides clothing and accessories, while a chain like Nilgiris specializes in food and bakery items.Shoppers' Stop targets the elite urban class, while Pantaloons is targeted at the middle class.

2. Breaking Bulk: Breaking bulk is another function performed by retailing. The word retailing is derived from the French word *retaillie,* meaning 'to cut a piece off' or 'to break bulk'. A retailer, thus, can be a dealer or trader, who sells goods in small quantities. To reduce transportation costs, manufacturers and wholesalers typically ship large cartons of the produce which are then tailored by the retailers into smaller quantities to meet individual consumption needs.

3. Holding Stock: Retailers also offer the service of holding stock for the manufacturers. Retailers maintain an inventory that allows for instant availability of the product to the consumers. It helps to keep prices stable and enables the manufacturer to regulate production. Consumers can keep a small stock of products at home as they know that this can be replenished by the retailer and can save on inventory carrying cost.

4. Additional Services: Retailers handle the change in ownership of merchandise by providing services that make it convenient to buy and use products. Providing product guarantees, after-sales service, and dealing with consumer complaints are some of the services that add value to the actual product at the retailers' end. Retailers also offer credit and hire-purchase facilities to the customers to enable them to buy a product now and pay for it later. Retailers fill orders, promptly process, deliver and install products. Salespeople are also employed by retailers to answer queries and provide additional information about the displayed products. The display itself allows the consumer to see and test products before actual purchase. Retail essentially completes transactions with customers.

5. Channel of Communication: Retailers also act as the channel of communication and information between the suppliers and the consumers. From the advertisements, salespeople, and display, shoppers learn about the characteristics and features of a product or services offered. Manufacturers, in their turn, learn of sales forecasts, delivery delays, and consumer complaints. The manufacturer can then modify defective or unsatisfactory merchandise and services.

6. Transport and Advertising Functions: Small manufacturers can use retailers to provide assistance with transport, storage, advertising and prepayment of merchandise. This also works the other way round in case the number of retailers is small. The number of functions performed by a particular retailer has a direct relation to the percentage and volume of sales needed to cover both their costs and profits.

CHARACTERISTIC FEATURES OF RETAILING

Retailing can be distinguished in various ways from other businesses such as manufacturing. Retailing differs from manufacturing in the following ways:

(i) Location is a critical factor in retail business.

(ii) There are a larger number of retail units compared to other members of the value chain. This occurs primarily to meet the requirements of geographical coverage and population density.

(iii) In most retail businesses services are as important as core products.

(iv) It is the only point in the value chain to provide a platform for promotions.

(v) A sale at the retail level is generally in smaller unit sizes.

(vi) There is direct end-user interaction in retailing.

The various characteristics features of retailing are:

Point-of-Purchase Display: A significant relevant chunk of retail sales comes from unplanned or impulse purchases. Therefore, display, point-of-purchase merchandise, store layout and catalogues become important. Impulse goods like chocolates, snack foods and magazines can sell much more quickly if they are placed in a high visibility and high traffic location.

Larger Number of Retail Business Units: Location of retail store plays an important role compared to other business units. Retailers consider factors like potential demand, supply of merchandise and store image-related factors in locating the retail outlet. The number of operating units in retail is the highest, primarily to meet the needs for geographic reach and customer accessibility.

Direct Interaction with Customers: Retail businesses have a direct interaction with end-users of goods or services. They act as intermediaries between consumers and suppliers who may be wholesalers or manufacturers. Therefore, they are in a position to effectively communicate the response and changing preferences of the consumers to the suppliers or salespersons of the company. This helps the manufacturers and marketers to redefine their product and change the components of its marketing strategy accordingly.

Lower Average Amount of Sales Transaction: Many consumers buy products in small quantities for household consumption. Due to lower disposable incomes, some consumer segments in India even buy grocery items on a daily basis rather than a weekly or a monthly basis. Inventory management becomes a challenge for retailers as a result of the many minor transactions with a large number of customers. Hence, retailers must take care in determining average levels of stock, order levels and the popularity of different brands.

RETAILER IN THE MARKETING CHANNEL

Channel is the path through which transfer of title is effected from the hands of manufacturer to the hands of ultimate consumer. With the growth of industrialization and urbanization, the distance between the manufacturer of the product and the actual consumer has increased. Many products are manufactured in one country and sold to a market in another. Most producers no longer sell their products directly to the consumer. They use intermediaries to get their products to the final consumer. The marketing channel design is largely based on the level of service desired by the target consumer. In consumer market retailer is working close to the ultimate consumer. The retailer provides valuable feedback to the manufacturer which helps to introduce product modification as per customers' changing taste and preferences.

The shortest consumer market channel is as follows

The channel clearly indicates that the retailer is acting as a connecting link between the manufacturer and consumer.

The traditional consumer market channel is as follows

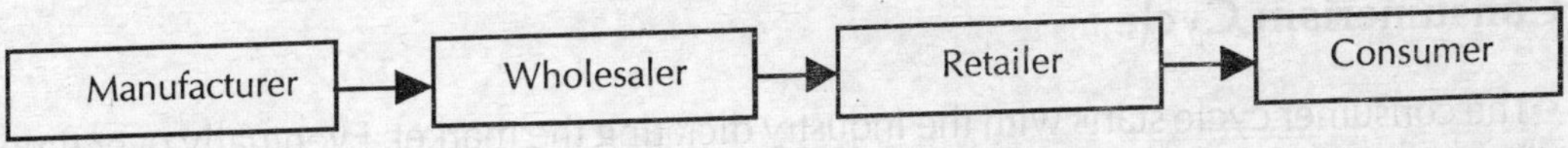

The traditional consumer market channel shows that retailer is working close to consumer rather than close to manufacturer. Hence in the consumer market the consumers mainly depend on their nearby retailer rather than the manufacturer to satisfy their dynamic needs and wants.

RETAILER AND MARKETING MIX

Marketing mix is defined as "the setting up of the decision variables or 4Ps, *viz.*, Product, Price, Promotion and Physical distribution at a particular point of time". Retailing which forms an integral part of the marketing mix includes elements like Product, Price, Promotion, Place, People and Presentation. Here place related to the distribution and availability of products in various locations. Thus in retail marketing, we concentrate on 6Ps.

Customers are first introduced to the product at the retail store. Organisations sell their products and services through these retail outlets and get feedback on the performance of their products and customers' expectations about them.

Retail stores serve as a communication hubs for customers. Point Of Sale(POS) and Point Of Purchase (POP) advertisement in retail stores transmit information to the customers. Hence, the role of retailing in the marketing mix is very significant.

In Retail marketing as a course, the learners are expected to know about the 6Ps namely,

- Product and Merchandise Management ***(Product)***
- Retail Consumer ***(People)***
- Retail Pricing ***(Price)***
- Retail Location, Planning, Design and Layout ***(Presentation)***
- Retail Channels ***(Place)***
- Retail Promotion and Communication ***(Promotion)***

MAIN DRIVES OF RETAILING IN INDIA

1. Raising Incomes

Over the past decade, India's middle-and high-income population has grown at a rapid pace of over 10% per annum. Though this growth is most evident in urban areas it has also taken place in rural markets. Further, the number of households with double earning is also on an increase. This growing high-income population is triggering the demand for consumer goods, leading to the proliferation of higher quality\higher priced products.

2. Consumerism Cycle

The consumer cycle starts with the industry dictating the market. Eventually over time the distributor gains control over the market; at this stage the distributor becomes an important link between manufacturer and consumer. When the market starts developing and expanding its horizons, retailers turn into the vital link in this supply chain. India is entering this third stage where retailers control the market. Being the closest link to the consumer in the supply chain, retailers benefit accordingly. Manufacturers spend a lot of money promoting a product, but if it's not on the shop-shelf, consumers won't be able to buy it. Manufacturers have also realized that retailer recommendations matter, particularly in smaller towns where retailers are figures of authority or opinion leaders. With shopping attitudes changing, the Indian market today desires value-added products and services with good ambience and brands, which only a retailer can provide. Hence good retailer relations are a must. Manufacturers are ready to pay listing fees to get retailers to stock a product, or display charges to place it prominently.

3. Establishment of the Supply Chain

Over the past few years, the consumer goods sector has been transformed by increased liberalization, continuous reduction in customs duty, a shift from quota to tariff-based systems for imports and sophistication in manufacturing. Entry restrictions for multinationals have been removed in nearly all sectors. All this has enabled chain retailers to enjoy better range depth and sourcing options as well as improved average margins. There has been a proliferation in the range across all categories, with a simultaneous increase in the supply of products and quality retail space. According to a study, there are over 18,000 stock-keeping units (SKUs) while most retailers have the space for only 5,000 - 7,000 units. This has tempted a number of real estate companies and other corporate into investing in malls and other retail formats.

4. Change in Consumer Behaviour

The urban woman today is literate and, in many cases, employed. There is greater work pressure and increased commuting time. And with a shift in the family structure, nuclear families have become a significant component of urban markets. According to a recent market research conducted in Bangaluru, the share of nuclear families is estimated to be as high as 70%. Besides all these factors, the increase in the variety, quality and availability of products, and higher spending power has led to the growing popularity of supermarkets. There has been a change in shopping behaviour in urban India over the past few years with customers looking for convenience. That is, they want everything under one roof and a bigger choice of products. With an increase in double-income households, people do not have much leisure time and seek the convenience of one-stop shopping in order to make the best use of their time. They also look for speed and efficiency. Increased awareness has also meant that consumers now seek more information, variety, product availability, better quality and hygiene as well as increased customer service. The concept of "Value for Money" is picking up.

Traditionally, children seldom accompanied their parents while shopping for groceries. Shopping for children was confined to festivals when dresses were bought for them. But now, because they are pressed for time, working parents prefer to spend as much time as possible with their children; this includes their shopping hours also. As malls and supermarkets offer the option of entertainment along with shopping, younger couples prefer to shop there. Also driving the retail industry is impulse buying spurred on by higher brand awareness.

Consumer niches have begun propelling the market and are becoming more important, with positive and negative sub-segments of consumers gaining significance. The growth accelerator has definitely been the working woman, with the money spent by her averaging 1.3 times that of a housewife.

5. Consumer Pull

In the pre-liberalisation, supply-led market, the power rested clearly with the manufacturers. In today's demand-led market, it's the consumer who calls the shots. Over the last decade, there has been a significant evolution in the Indian consumer, mainly due to the liberalisation of the consumer goods industry that was initiated in the mid-eighties and accelerated through the nineties, combined with a growing consumerism driven by the media, new opportunities and increasing wealth. Although this change is most noticeable in the metros, it has affected consumers in smaller towns as well.

6. New Entrepreneurs

The growing attractiveness of the retail trade has begun to attract new entrepreneurs with ideas, and venture capitalists with funds. Subhiksha, an innovative discount grocery chain in Chennai, has expanded to a total of 50 stores in less than three years, and is one of the most successful retail start-ups of the recent past. Venture capitalists like ICICI also increasingly willing to invest in retail businesses.

7. Explosion of Media

There has been an explosion in media as well, during the past decade, kick-started by the cable explosion during the Gulf War, television has accelerated to a point where there are more cable connections than telephones in Indian homes and about 90 channels are being aired at all times. This media bombardment has exposed the Indian consumer to the lifestyles of more affluent countries and raised their aspirations and expectations from the shopping experience – they want more choice, value, service, experience and convenience.

8. Foreign Retailers Looking for Entry Options

The increasing attractiveness of the sector has drawn the interest of a number of global retailers. With the opening up of the economy, more and more MNCs have entered the Indian business arena through joint ventures, franchisees or even self-owned store. The very first MNC to get into the business was Spencer's, a tie-up between the RPG Group and Dairy Farm International, a $10 billion Hong Kong company. While foreign retailers cannot start operations on their own mainly because of FDI restrictions on the sector, in apparel, Benetton, Lifestyle, etc., are starting retailing joint venture in India.

9. Technological Impact

Technology is probably the most dynamic change agent in the retailing industry. The computerisation of the various operations in a retail store – including inventory management, billing and payment as well as database (of customers) management – widespread use of bar coding, point-of-sale terminals and Management Information System has changed the face of retailing drastically. Technology not only provides timely information but also prevents theft and promotes in-store appearance. Technology makes the customers life a lot easier through debit cards, credit cards and smart cards.

10. Building Chains Around Brands

Apparel, footwear and consumer durable brands have driven the growth of specially chains and upgraded existing multi-brand outlets. Many emerging large retailers like Titan, Raymonds developed their retailing business through their brands. Thus, there is consumer brand seeking than product seeking in stores.

11. Expansion of Family-Owned Businesses

The most successful of these are the ₹ 150 crore Viveks, the 40-years old Chennai consumer durables chain, the ₹ 50 crore Pantaloon apparel retail business, and Bangaluru's food retailer Nilgiris. This gradually compels the local small retailers transforming into supermarkets. Managing inventory in a small space and keeping low turnover is also becoming difficult. Hence, moving up to newer business opportunities and creating the space for a new model will take top priority.

12. Awareness in Rural Market

The rural market is beginning to emerge as an important consumption area, accounting for over one-third of the demand for most key consumer durables and non-durable products. In response, manufacturers of consumer goods have begun developing new products and marketing strategies with the rural consumer in mind.

13. Emergence of Hubs of Retail Activity

Chennai, Bangaluru and Hyderabad have become major retail hubs. In Chennai about 20% of food sales flow through supermarkets and 25-30% of consumer durable sales come from speciality chains such as Viveks and Vasanth.

14. Change in Scale of Operations

Subhiksha has over 50 stores in Chennai and Food World has 41, spread over Chennai, Bangaluru and Hyderabad. The growing scale enables the supermarkets to eliminate links in purchasing chain and to make deals with food processors directly. For example, Hindustan Lever Limited (HLL), one of the India's largest consumer goods company supply directly to the retailers operating with a special team.

15. Entry of the Corporate Sector

Due to the fast development of retail sector even big corporate houses like Tata, Birla and Reliance has entered into retailing. Big business houses in India today are in the position to provide the Indian masses with shopping satisfaction, quality products, product information and discounts. Retail store remain popular in the minds of consumer because of their social interaction, variety offering and polite salespersons.

RETAILING IN INDIA

Retailing is one of the pillars of the economy in India and accounts for 35% of GDP. Over 12 million outlets operate in the country and only 4% of them being larger than 500 sq ft in size. Most Indian shopping takes place in open markets and in millions of independent grocery shops. Indian market has high complexities in terms of a wide geographic spread and distinct consumer preferences varying by each region necessitating a need for localization even within the geographic zones. India has highest number of retail outlets per person. It is around 11 per thousand people. The traditional grocers, by introducing self-service formats as well as value-added services such as credit and home delivery, have tried to redefine themselves. However, the boom in retailing has been confined primarily to the urban markets in the country.

While barter is considered as the oldest form of retail trade, since independence retail in India has evolved to support the unique needs of the country, given its size and complexity. Early retailing in India can be traced back to the weekly haats or gatherings at the market place and melas, where not only the local products, but also products from outside used to be on display for sale. They still continue to present in most part of the country and form an essential part of life and trade in various areas. Later on, local mom-and-pop stores (kirana stores) sprung up in the landscape to cater to the needs of the local population. Hence, the early Indian retail scenario was primarily dominated by local products and local vendors. There were no branded products at that time. The local manufacturer simply used to put up his wares for sale. Although this trading of goods was going on for ages, yet only in the recent past the buying and selling of goods has become more of finesse and brand dominated activity.

Since liberalisation, the Indian economy slowly progressed from being state led to become market friendly. This is the beginning of a new era for retail in India. The emergence of the modern Indian housewife, who managed her home and work, led to a demand for more products, a better shopping ambience, more convenience and one stop shopping. Hence, retailers have started providing some pleasant enjoyable experience to the consumers by providing improved facilities like shopping ambience, friendly layout and a single point-of-purchase laced with the lure of discounts. The modern, systematic and consumer oriented shopping culture is the mainstay of organised retailing. This fuelled the growth of supermarkets, hypermarkets, departmental stores, malls, etc.

Organised retailing appeared in the Indian horizon in the 70s when shops like Raymond's, Nalli and Bata set up their exclusive stores and / or franchisees. The early 80s witnessed the emergence of "Akbarally's" in Mumbai and "Spencer's" in Chennai. These stores later evolved into multi-chain outlets and were the first to establish the concept of organised retail in India. During the 90s, with the opening up of the Indian economy through Liberalisation, Privatisation and Globalisation, new retailing formats and exclusive outlets like Shoppers' Stop (1991) and Pantaloon (1997) appeared in India.

Towards the end of the 20th century, Indian retailing underwent a sea change with the opening up of numerous supermarkets, department stores, chain stores, hypermarkets, big discount stores and malls throughout the length and breadth of the country. The booming of the retail sector opened up new vistas so much so that this sector is now treated as the sunrise sector with prospects of unlimited growth. National players like Tata, RPG, ITC, Reliance, etc., are cashing on this booming sector. Therefore, the country is witnessing introduction of many modern formats and techniques, which are changing the retail landscape for most of the product categories.

In India, retailing is the buzz word now-a-days. This sector has modernized and expanded at a rapid pace in synchronization with India's economic growth. Retail industry is continuously going through changes on account of liberalisation, globalisation and consumer preferences. While multinational retail chains are looking for new markets, manufacturer are identifying, redefining or evolving new retail formats. The existing retail houses are also gearing up to face the emerging competition from the organised sector and the changing outlook of the consumers. For example, consumer spending is shifting from goods to services. Accordingly, the retailers too are fast adjusting to the changing consumer preferences.

Consumers are not only looking for the core products or functional benefits from the retailers but also the non-functional benefits, which need to be compatible with their lifestyles. For example, most of the traditional eating joints in India such as Haldiram, Ananda Bhavan have revised their product offerings and atmospherics on the lines of the multinational chains to compete with them and to serve changed expectations of the consumers. The retail sector is changing as new store categories have started dominating the marketplace. Mass merchandisers(Wal-Mart, Big Bazaar), discount clubs (Subhiksha), so-called category killers (Home Depot, Vishal chain) and speciality retailers (Time Zone, Tanishq) have all developed successful retail models.

In the Indian context the various studies conducted regarding retailing in India reveals the following:

- In India, the major drives for a grocery stores is nearness to the place of residence and the comfort level that the customer has in dealing with the store owner like personal relationship.
- The Indian consumers are price sensitives so the retailers have to manage with razor thin margins in order to compete in the competitive grocery store market.
- Indian retailers understand the culture, taste and preference of the Indian consumers better than others.
- In food and grocery retail sector, it was found that customer's loyalty in grocery stores was found to be positively related to location, cleanliness, quality, helpful and trustworthy salespeople, home shopping, *etc.*
- Seasonality affect apparel sector so the retailer has to clear of the stock at the end of the season. So the apparel retailer use ends of season sale twice in a year where discount is given up to 50 per cent of the Maximum Retail Price (MRP).
- If customer is satisfied with the product and service they will come again to the retail shop. The customers show their interest to visit organised retail malls. Every retail shop wants to create their target customer.

ORGANISED RETAILING IN INDIA

After agriculture, retail is the second largest employer in India. But in India, retail sector is fragmented and consists of predominantly small, independent and owner managed shops. There is a boom in the retail trade in India owing to a gradual increase in the disposable income of the middle class household. The local kirana stores are growing at the rate of 8% per annum but the need for retailing is growing at a rate of 15% per annum. As the local stores are not able to satisfy the total demand, more and more players are coming in the market with new attractive retail formats like supermarkets, hypermarkets, departmental stores, malls, *etc.* These organised retail sectors are keeping almost all convenience goods under one roof which attracts more customers. More number of national and international players are entering into the Indian organised retail sector. So the organised retail sector is becoming large. The Indian market is currently witnessing a retail boom with organised retailers offering a whole assortment of goods to consumers under one roof with congenial shopping ambience. Modern organised retailing competes based on the price and variety. They also exploit the fact that due to the hectic lives and changing lifestyle, today's consumer simply doesn't have as much time as before to do the shopping.

With liberalisation, privatisation, globalisation and modernisation, a modern competitive business is based on understanding the mind of the consumer and providing the kind of products and services that he wants. Considering the truth that the customer is the king, every organisation wants to increase market share and profit. The competitors are also following the same strategy. So, all of them try to get more customers which leads to increased market share and profit through different marketing activities. If the customers'wants matches with what the companies are offering, then the company will succeed.

Indian organised retailing is under transition today, bringing a lot of changes in the formats of retailing. The shoppers enjoy the privilege of shopping the goods and services required by them in variety of formats. The shoppers are exposed to various formats of shopping ranging from local kirana's shop, convenience stores, supermarkets and hypermarkets. The growth of retailing in India has impact on formats. While the traditional models of retailing-street-end pan shop, kirana shop, fancy shop and department store continue, the new formats like supermarkets, malls, hypermarkets and speciality stores are running parallel.

The retail industry is divided into organised and unorganised sectors. Organised retailing refers to trading activities undertaken by licensed retailers, that is, those who are registered for sales tax, income tax, *etc*. These include the corporate-backed hypermarkets and retail chains, and also the privately owned large retail businesses. Organised retailing in India initially began in the south. The availability of land at prime locations with lower realestate price compared to north made multistoried shopping complexes possible. In south India Chennai, Bangaluru and Hyderabad has emerged as a centre of organised retailing. In Chennai nearly 20% of food sales is accounted for by supermarkets and an equal share of consumer durables is sold through speaciality chains like Vivek's. This concept of shopping took route in major cities like Mumbai and Delhi after 2 years following the south.

Organised retailing got a fillip in 2004 with the opening of new format stores, new generation shopping malls, FDI investment in retail and formation of Retailer's Association of India. The booming economy led to higher purchasing power of the consumers and market for consumer durables, clothing, automobiles, telecom products, etc. India is rapidly evolving into an exciting and competitive market place with potential target consumers in both the rich and middle class segment. Organised retailing are springing up in urban areas to market consumer goods in a style similar to that of malls. Even though big retail chains like Shopper's Stop are concentrating on upper segment and selling their product at higher prices some other big retailers like Food World and Big Bazers tapping the huge middle class population. Over the years international brands like MacDonalds and Pepsi invaded and thrived in India. Retailing is one of the fastest growing industry in India, catering to the world's second largest consumer market. However, the boom in organised retailing has been confined primarily to the urban markets.

Unorganised retailing refers to the traditional formats of low-cost retailing, for example, the local grocery shops, owner manned general stores, convenience stores, handcart and pavement vendors, *etc.* It took ten years for the first 2,500 organised retail stores to emerge in India. Organized retailing accounts for just 4% of the market as of 2008. Even there, large chunks are yet to feel the impact of organised retailing. There are two primary reasons for this. First, the modern retailer is yet to feel the saturation effect in the urban market and has, therefore, probably not looked at the other markets as seriously. Second, the modern retailing trend, despite its cost-effectiveness, has come to be identified with lifestyles. Organised retailing has definitely made headway in the upper class. However, even in this segment, items such as milk, fruits, vegetables and a significant portion of 'through-the-month' purchases seem to be done at traditional outlets. The middle income class prefer shopping for processed food and personal care in supermarkets and fall back on traditional outlets for bulk shopping. Organised retail outlets seem to be associated with branded items/special purchases. Organised retailing does not seem to have made an impact on the lower class, except for 'curiosity' shopping. The biggest question before organised retailers therefore, is whether this really means a huge untapped potential for the organised retailers and whether, the conversion in mindset is going to be easy.

Retailing, one of the largest sectors in the global economy, is going through a transition phase not only in India but the world over. For a long time, the corner grocery store was the only choice available to the consumer. This is slowly giving way to international formats of retailing. The traditional food and grocery segment has seen the emergence of supermarkets/ grocery chains (Food World, Nilgiris, Apna Bazaar), convenience stores (ConveniO, HP Speedmart) and fast-food chains (McDonalds, Dominos). It is the non-food segment, however, that foray has been made into a variety of new sectors. These include lifestyle/fashion segments (Shoppers' Stop, Globus, LifeStyle, Westside), apparel/accessories (Pantaloon, Levis, Reebok), books/music/gifts (Archies, Music World, Crosswords, Landmark), appliances and consumer durables (Viveks, Vasanth & Co.), drugs and pharmacy (Health and Glow, Apollo). The emergence of new sectors has been accompanied by changes in existing formats as well as the beginning of new formats. Retail marketing in India on the basis of their size can be classified as

- Hyper markets above 50,000 sq. ft.
- Large supermarkets, typically 25,000-50,000 sq. ft.
- Mini supermarkets, typically 1,000-2,000 sq. ft.
- Convenience stores, typically 750-1,000 sq. ft.

The traditional grocers, by introducing self-service formats as well as value-added services such as credit and home delivery, have tried to redefine themselves. In order to appeal to all classes of the society, retail stores would have to identify with different lifestyles. In a sense, this trend is already visible with the emergence of stores with an essentially 'value for money' image. The attractiveness of the other stores actually appeals to the existing affluent class as well as those who aspire to be part of this class. Hence, one can assume that the retailing revolution is emerging along the lines of the economic evolution of society.

Organised retailing is spreading and making its presence felt in different parts of the country. The trend in grocery retailing, however, has been slightly different with a growth concentration in the South. Chennai which was considered a 'traditional', conservative' and 'cost-conscious' market, proved to be the home ground for most of the successful retail names - Food World, Music World, Health and Glow, Vasanth, Subhiksha and Viveks-to name a few.

The choice of Chennai as the 'retail capital' has surprised many, but a variety of factors acted in its favour. Chennai, in spite of being a rapidly growing metropolis offers reasonable real estate prices, one of the most critical elements for the industry. Chennai has been witnessing a high industrial growth and increasing presence of the MNCs, both in the IT sector as well as outside it. The industrial boom has led to the emergence of new residential areas with aggregation of professionals as well as a rapid increase in the number of 'double-income' households and growth of the rich/upper middle class with increased purchasing power. All the factors have acted favourably in nurturing the retail industry.

GROWTH DRIVES OF ORGANISED RETAILING IN INDIA

The phenomenal growth in the retail sector in India can be attributed mainly to:

1. The booming Indian economy.
2. Increasing proportion of young working population.
3. Increase in the number of working women providing for double income households.
4. Changing value orientations of the population from austerity to conspicuous consumption.
5. Increasing use of debit cards and credit cards.
6. Rapid urbanisation.
7. Provides an alternative investment opportunity.
8. Tremendous scope for expansion in Tier II cities.
9. Sectors with High Growth Potential: Food and Grocery (91 per cent), Clothing (55 per cent), Furniture and Fixtures (27 per cent), Pharmacy (27 per cent), Durables, Footwear and Leather, Watch and Jewellery (18 per cent) are poised for very high growth in coming years.
10. Retailing in Rural Areas: Retail sector offers opportunities for exploration, expansion and investment in rural areas, in spite of the fact that some of the Corporates and Entrepreneurs earlier have made a foray into it. ITC launched the country's first rural

mall 'Chaupal Sagar', offering a diverse product range from FMCGs to electronic appliances to automobiles, attempting to provide the farmers with a one-stop destination for all their needs. There has been yet another initiative by the DCM Sriram Group called the 'Hariyali Bazzar' that initially started off by providing farm related inputs and services but plans to introduce the complete shopping basket in due course of time. Other corporate bodies include Escorts and Tata Chemicals (with Tata Kisan Sansar) setting up agri-stores to provide product/services targeted at the farmer in order to tap the vast rural market.

TRENDS AND OPPORTUNITIES FOR ORGANISED RETAILING IN INDIA

- Even though India has well over 5 million retail outlets of all sizes and styles, the country sorely lacks anything that can resemble a retailing industry in the modern sense of the term. This presents international retailing specialists with a great opportunity.
- As much as 96 per cent of the 5 million-plus outlets are smaller than 500 square feet in area. This means that Indias, per capita retailing space is about 2 square feet (compared to 16 square feet in the United States). India's per capita retailing space is thus the lowest in the world
- Just over 8 per cent of India's population is engaged in retailing (compared to 20 per cent in the United States).
- Given the size, and the geographical, cultural and socio-economic diversity of India, there is no role model for Indian suppliers and retailers to adapt or expand in the Indian context.
- The first challenge facing the organised retail industry in India is competition from the unorganised sector. Traditional retailing was established in India for some centuries. It is a low cost structure, mostly owner-operated, has negligible real estate and labour costs and little or no taxes to pay. Consumer familiarity that runs from generation to generation is one big advantage for the traditional retailing sector. But they are growing only at 8% p.a. whereas the need for retailing growth is 15% p.a.
- Players in the organised sector have big expenses to meet, and yet have to keep prices low enough to be able to compete with the traditional sector. High costs for the organised sector arises from: higher labour costs, social security to employees, high quality real estate, much bigger premises, comfort facilities such as air-conditioning, back-up power supply, taxes, *etc.* Organised retailing also has to cope with the middle class psychology that the bigger and brighter a sales outlet is, the more expensive it will be.
- The above should not be seen as a gloomy foreboding from global retail operators. International retail majors such as Benetton, Dairy Farm and Levis have already entered the market. Lifestyles in India are changing and the concept of "value for money" is picking up.

- India's first true shopping mall – complete with food courts, recreation facilities and large car parking space – was inaugurated as lately as in 1999 in Mumbai. (This mall is called "Crossroads").
- Local companies and local-foreign joint ventures are expected to more advantageously postioned than the purely foreign ones in capturing organised India's retailing industry, in India and benefit from it.
- The prospects are very encouraging. The first steps towards sophisticated retailing are being taken, and "Crossroads" is the best example of this awakening. More such malls have been planned in the other big cities of India.

While the retailing industry itself has been present through history in our country, it is only the recent past that has witnessed so much dynamism. It is the latest bandwagon that has witnessed hordes of players leaping onto it. The emergence of retailing in India has more to do with the increasing purchasing power of buyers, specially post- liberalisation, increase in product variety, and the increasing economies of scale, with the aid of modern supply and distribution management solutions.

The current retailing revolution has been provided an impetus from multiple sources. These 'revolutionaries' include many conventional stores upgrading themselves to modern retailing, companies in competitive environments entering the market directly to ensure exclusive visibility for their products and professional chain stores coming up to meet the need of the manufacturers. Attractiveness, accessibility and affordability seem to be the key offerings of the retailing chain.

Retailing in India has a very long haul ahead. The process of getting into newer forms of purchasing has been gradual because of traditional buying habit and the manner in which traditional retailers manage relationship. There is no specific international format or existing role model that can be easily adopted and applied in the India context. The growth and development of organised retailing in India will be driven by two factors namely low price and benefits the consumer cannot resist. Economies of scale will help the retailers to bring down the cost and increase the benefits offered to the consumer. The key drivers for growth of organized retailing in India are

- Growing consumerism paving the way for greater consumer enlightenment.
- Liberalised economic platform enabling the entry of global retailers to set up shop in India through joint ventures, franchisees *etc.*
- Expansion of organized retailing through scaling up to minimize cost and increase margin.

MAJOR INDIAN RETAILORS

Indian apparel retailers are increasing their brand presence overseas, particularly, in developed markets. While most have identified a gap in countries in West Asia and Africa, some majors are also looking at the US and Europe. Arvind Brands, Madura Garments, Spykar Lifestyle and Royal Classic Polo are busy chalking out foreign expansion plans through the distribution route and standalone stores as well. Another denim wear brand, Spykar, which is now moving towards becoming a casualwear lifestyle brand, has launched its store in Melbourne.

The low-intensity entry of the diversified Mahindra Group into retail is unique because it plans to focus on lifestyle products. The Mahindra group is the fourth large Indian business group to enter the business of retail after Reliance Industries Ltd, the Aditya Birla Group, and Bharti Enterprises Ltd. The other three groups are focusing either on perishables and groceries, or a range of products, or both.

- Vivek Limited Retail Formats: Viveks, Jainsons, Viveks Service Centre, Viveks Safe Deposit Lockers
- REI AGRO LTD Retail-Formats:6Ten Hyper and 6Ten Super
- RPG Retail-Formats: Music World, Books & Beyond, Spencer's Hyper, Spencer's Super, Daily & Fresh
- Pantaloon Retail-Formats: Big Bazaar, Food Bazaar, Pantaloons, Central, Fashion Station, Brand Factory, Depot, aLL, E-Zone *etc.*
- The Tata Group-Formats: Westside, Star India Bazaar, Steeljunction, Landmark, Titan Industries with World of Titans showrooms, Tanishq outlets, Chroma.
- K Raheja Corp Group-Formats: Shopper's Stop, Crossword, Hyper City, Inorbit
- Lifestyle International-Lifestyle, Home Centre, Max, Fun City and International Franchise brand stores.
- Pyramid Retail-Formats: Pyramid Megastore, TruMart
- Nilgiri's-Formats: Nilgiris' supermarket chain
- Subhiksha-Formats: Subhiksha supermarket pharmacy and telecom discount chain.
- Trinethra- Formats: Fabmall supermarket chain and Fabcity hypermarket chain
- Vishal Retail Group-Formats: Vishal Mega Mart
- BPCL-Formats: In and Out
- Reliance Retail-Formats: Reliance Fresh
- Reliance ADAG Retail-Format: Reliance World
- German Metro Cash and Carry
- Shoprite Holdings-Formats: Shoprite Hyper
- Aditya Birla Group - more Outlets

IMPACT OF ECONOMIC SLOWDOWN ON INDIAN RETAILING

The organised retail business in India has been affected by economic downturn, raising unemployment, inflation and the consumer's unwillingness to spend. This has resulted in lower sales, and in some cases, retail outlets have also had to be shutdown. Several corporate entrants into India's retail sector including the Aditya Birla Group, Pantaloon Retail, RPG Group's Spencer's Retail, Reliance and Vishal Retail among others have been affected by the reduced rate of economic growth.

According to the Indian retail sector outlook 2009 by Fitch Research, the Indian retail industry has been affected over the past year by various factors including slow economic growth, high interest rates and liquidity crunch. The industry was also affected by the high cost of real estate rents. Most retailers experienced a drop in footfall and demand, reflecting in slowing store sales and in a greater time to break even. The crisis in consumer confidence and discretionary purchases has had a major effect on retail strategies.

Change in Consumer Buying Behaviour

Consumers have changed their spending priorities. They are taking care of their needs, rather than their wants. In order to be successful, it is important for the retailer to respond to the nuances of the changing consumer mood. Consumer's commitment to helping themselves and their families survive hard times overrides any other loyalty.

Retailers should help the consumers to achieve these goals. So the retailers have to provide consumers with the right kind of product at the right price and create brand loyalty. This is also the right time for the retailer to focus on long term plans and to larger market share, as weaker players disappeared.

Decline in Footfalls in Retail Stores

The number of consumers frequenting shopping malls and large department stores has also decreased considerably. Malls have been adopting different promotional campaigns to attract customers.

For the retailers, innovative Customer Relationship Management (CRM) activities are the need of the hour along with different product ranges catering to the changing needs of the customers. Value for money products will sell, as the customer is looking for long term investment and not just short term delight.

Heavy Toll on Jobs

The retail sector employs 24 million people, but only 500,000 work in the organised sector. While there are no official numbers on retail job losses, industry experts say it is around 15%.

This is, however, the right time for the retailers to pick and choose the right talent so as to bring in fresh energy and insights. Gaining employees' loyalty through internal marketing and looking for talent within the organisation are some ways for optimizing the productivity of shop floor employees.

Decline in Sales

Major departmental stores like Shoppers' Stop have experienced a decline in sales, prompting them to close some of their airport shops and food outlets. The Adithya Birla Group, which began retailing operations in 2007 after acquiring Hyderabad based Trinethra chain of stores, is believed to have incurred a net loss of ₹ 534 crore on the sales turnover of ₹ 1030 crore during 2008-09. Pantaloon Retail India Ltd., showed a decline in sales of household products and durables. Despite a healthy 21% rise in sales during the quarter ended March 31, 2009, it posted a less than expected rise in the net profit.Spencer's Retail, known mainly for food and grocery retail, made a foray into lifestyle retailing, but ended the year with no growth in 'same store sales.'

The solution to counter this problem is that big retailers take up private labels business more aggressively as the new mantra to beat the slowdown. This will enable them to leverage the benefits of branded products, while keeping the prices lower and more cost effective for consumers, rather than the corresponding national brands. Private labels offer better value for money to the consumers.

Many Stores are Shutting Shop

Retailers expanded without adequate backend logistics and supply chain, leaving the outlets vulnerable. High rentals, coupled with low returns and mounting interest rates, made once successful Subhiksha close 1200 stores across India. Reliance shut around 50 of its Reliance Fresh stores and laid off 13% of its 30,000 strong workforce.

It is time to enter into alliances or partnerships, manage stores more effectively, take help from experts and change product profiles to match customer needs. Diversify and move towards niche rather than mass markets. Renegotiate rentals, effective inventory management and cost cutting techniques making the front-line sales people more productive and cutting down marketing and advertising budgets.

Retail sector will recover and get back on track, in spite of the effects of the economic slowdown. Consumer will emerge as the king, compelling the retailers to make necessary changes in order to survive.

FUTURE OF RETAIL IN INDIA

In India, the retail sector is the second largest employer after agriculture. The retailing sector in India is highly fragmented and consists predominantly of small, independent and owner-managed shops. There are some 12 million retail outlets in India. Besides, the country is also dotted with low-cost kiosks and pushcarts. There has been a boom in the retail trade in India owing to a gradual increase in the disposable income of the middle-class households. More and more players are venturing into the retail business in India to introduce new attractive retail formats like malls, supermarkets, discount stores, department stores and even changing the traditional look of the bookstores, chemist shops and furnishing stores. Food sales constitute a high proportion of the total retail sales. However, the non-food retailing sector registered faster year-on-year growth than food sales.

The retail business in India is expected to expand widely with further growth of organised retailing in both food and non-food segments. The proportion of sales through organised retailing is estimated to increase to around 6% by 2010 which presently account for only 4%. The Indian retail market, which is the fifth largest retail destination globally, is estimated to grow to 427 billion US dollars by 2010 and 637 billion US dollars by 2015. A strong trend in favour of organised retail format is being witnessed in both food and non-food sectors as people are showing preference of one-stop shops. Customers are also looking for convenience in shopping.

In future, with more dual income families, the consumer's ability to spend will increase, but at the same time, it is predicted that the time available for shopping will go down. In such scenario, the retailers will have to take steps to develop shopping as an experience, through the more successful retailers will be those that will provide faster services.

The shopping mall phenomenon is not likely to be restricted only to metros as malls are also coming up in non-metro cities and larger towns across the country. It is stated that there are immense opportunities and possibilities for mall developers and retailers to explore beyond metros. The growing consumer needs in the mini metros, Tier II and Tier III cities are almost matching up to that in the metros. Nearly a decade after the first signs of organised retail format evolution, India is expecting to, develop vast retail real estate space. India has one of the largest number of retail outlets in the world. Still, organized retails accounts for only 4% of the total market, opening huge growth potential in this segment. India represents an economic opportunity on a massive scale, both as a global base and as a domestic market. Retailing business is playing a major role throughout the world, increasing productivity across a wide range of consumer goods and services. Its fruits have been witnessed by many developed nations like USA, UK and Mexico. The retail sector is slowly developing in India and its impact has also started in India. This is happening due to the Indian consumer class. The modernization of the Indian retail sector will be reflected in the rapid growth in sales in supermarkets, departmental stores and hypermarkets. This is because of the growing preference of the affluent and upper middle classes for shopping at these types of retail stores, given the conveniences they offer such as shopping ambience, varity and a single-point source of purchase.

CHALLENGES TO RETAIL DEVELOPMENT IN INDIA

Organized retail in India is little over a decade old. It is largely an urban phenomenon and the pace of growth is still slow. Some of the reasons for this slow growth are:

1. Retail not Recognised as an Industry in India

Lack of recognition as an industry hampers the availability of finance to the existing and new players. This affects growth and expansion plans.

2. The High Costs of Real Estate

Real estate prices in some cities in India are among the highest in the world. The lease or rent of the property is one of the major areas of expenditure; high lease rentals eat into the profitability of a project.

3. High Stamp Duties

In addition to the high cost of real estate, the sector also faces very high stamp duties on transfer of property, which varies from state to state (12.5% in Gujarat and 8% in Delhi). The presence of strong pro-tenancy laws makes it difficult to evict tenants. The problem is compounded by problems of clear titles to ownership, while at the same time land use conversion is time consuming and complex as are legal processes for settling of property disputes.

4. Lack of Adequate Infrastructure

Poor roads and the lack of a cold chain infrastructure hampers the development of food and fresh grocery retail in India. The existing supermarkets and food retailers have to invest a substantial amount of money and time in building a cold chain network.

5. Multiple and Complex Taxation System

The sales tax rates vary from state to state, while organised players have to face a multiple point control and tax system, there is considerable sales tax evasion by small stores. In many locations, retailers have to face a multi point octroi. With the introduction of Value Added Tax (VAT) in 2005, certain anomalies in the existing sales tax system causing disruptions in the supply chain are likely to get corrected over a period of time.

6. Threat of New Entrants

In the case of the Indian retail sector, there exists a high threat of new entrants as the sector itself is in a nascent stage and is growing. Limited barriers to entry exist.

7. Threat of Substitutes

In Indian retail, the threat of substitutes is very high. The unorganized retailing in India is still the largest wherein cheaper versions of products are available. This still services most of the middle and poor income families in the country.

8. Bargaining Power of Suppliers

The price at which the product is available to the retailer for selling to the end consumer is very important in retail, as it plays a large role in the actual profitability.The suppliers to the retailing industry are the companies who provide the finished products to make various retail products. The bargaining power of suppliers is low because there are a large number of potential suppliers in the market. Therefore the prices become competitive. The emergence of private labels in apparel and food has infact played a key role in controlling the bargaining power of suppliers.

9. Bargaining Power of Buyers

In Indian retail, the bargaining power of buyers is fast increasing and can be termed as moderate to high, depending on the product or service. The buyers are the most powerful in the retailing industry. In an age of the informed consumer, meeting the buyer's expectations in terms of product, price and service is increasingly becoming difficult.

10. Intensity of Rivalry

The intensity of rivalry between competitors in an industry depends on the structure of competition – for example, rivalry is more intense where there are many small or equally sized competitors; rivalry is less when an industry has a clear market leader. The competition among the existing firms in the Indian market is not very high as there are few players in the market. High product differentiation is a major factor that intensifies the competition.

11. Technology

Most of the organised retailers are using available and affordable technology to capture consumer information. Modern retailers are using scanned data to figure out the answers to a lot of questions. Through technology, retailers can capture a whole lot of segmentation variables and subsequently use them for shopper segmentation. Technology helps to take better decisions in some critical areas such as new product introduction, suitable product offering, quicker ordering and assortment planning. Retailers use shopper's loyalty data to design customized promotional offering for different set of customers.

12. Human Resources

At present talent is in short supply and employee churn has been high for all players. It is very difficult to get experienced stores managers to run stores. The retailer is ready with retail space in different malls and high traffic retail location but availability of qualified and experienced personnel is still a big concern for the retailer. Almost all retailers resort to poaching which is at best a temporary solution. In view of the rapid expansion of retail business in India, retaining and developing workforce is of utmost importance to supply a talent pool to cater to the needs of this sunrise sector.

13. Store Positioning

The success of any retail business depends upon attracting and retaining the customer base. Therefore, retail stores should position themselves in such a way so that customers would find it convenient to come to their retail store. If store position is not done in a proper location, the success ratio does not improve. Big international players like Nanz failed to take because of their improper positioning, they targeted the upper end of the market and they could not survive. They faded away from the retail scenario in India. In the same line, Indian players like Subiksha and Big Bazaar are able to attain success through "value proportion" positioning.

14. Foreign Direct Investment

Though talk of opening up of the retail sector for FDI has been going on for quite sometime, no major break through has taken place in retail sector so far. FDI would bring a lot of positive changes both for the operators and the consumers. The infusion of much-needed foreign investment would result in retail consolidation, increasing supply chain efficiency, flow of technical know-how and global practices. It will make shoppers feel that they are having an informative shopping experience.

To summarise, the retail sector in India is a highly fragmented sector. In India, it is characterized by low entry barriers, the absence of economies of scale, high transportation costs and diverse market needs. Retailers need to take these factors into consideration and work towards creating economies of scale. Retailing is a dynamic field which requires dynamic individuals to implement innovative, dynamic retail programmes that will generate significant returns to the retailers.

Questions

I. Fill in the Blanks

1. Retailing includes all activities involved in selling goods to the final _________ .
2. In retailing SKU means____________.
3. Majority of the retail business in India is __________
4. Organised retailing in India initially began in ___________India
5. Organised retailing in India are springing up in _____________ areas.

Answers

1.consumer 2. Stock Keeping Unit 3. unorganised. 4. South 5. urban

II. Choose the Best Answer

1. The word retailing is derived from the French word *retaillie* which means ______

   (a) to cut (b) to break bulk (c) to sell (d) to trade

2. __________ is a critical factor in retail business

   (a) Store site (b) Finance (c) Location (d) Merchandise

3. Retail business has a direct interaction with the __________

   (a) end user (b) seller (c) trader (d) manufacturer

4. In India the retail sector is the ________ largest employer

   (a) third (b) fourth (c) first (d) second

5. __________ is the retail capital

   (a) Mumbai (b) Chennai (c) Delhi (d) Bangaluru

Answers

1. b 2. c 3. a 4. d 5. b

III. Answer in One Word

1. What is retailing?
2. What are the 6Ps in retail marketing?
3. How Indian retail industry is divided?
4. What is unorganized retailing?
5. Mention any five major retailers in India.

IV. Essay Questions

1. Define retailing. What are the functions of a retailer?
2. Discuss about the main drives of retailing in India?
3. Explain organized retailing in India.
4. Discuss about the trends and opportunities for organized retailing in India
5. Explain the challenges to retail development in India

Chapter 2

RETAIL CONSUMER

INTRODUCTION

Retailers need to research who their customers are and how their customers make decisions. Retailers cannot rely only on institution. The accurate understanding of consumer needs, helps the retailer to place the right product in the hands of consumer. For the retailer, there is a need to understand the different ways in which consumers choose and evaluate alternative retail services. Retailers need to know the various influences that lead the consumer to purchase, not just the store from where the purchase was made. Hence, the retailer must understand the various external and internal influences. The retailer must be aware of

- The purchase motives of individuals
- How demographic change affect retail purchasing
- Effect of various promotional tactics
- The complexity of purchase decision
- The different market segments based upon purchase behaviour
- How the retailer can improve their chance of success

Understanding the consumer behaviour completely may not be possible, but a retailer can know his customer. Any successful retail establishment understands its customers, how they think and behave, where they live, and their demographic characteristics. All retailing tactics should be directed towards those customers who will inevitably purchase the products and services offered. It will also help the retailer to price their product in such a way which will satisfy the customer and at the same time generate a profit to the store.

TYPES OF BUYING DECISIONS

The buying process begins when customers recognise an unsatisfied need. Then they seek information about how to satisfy the need: what products might be useful and how they can be bought. Customers evaluate the various alternative sources of merchandise such as stores, catalogs, and the Internet and choose a store or an internet site to visit or a catalog to review. This encounter with a retailer provides more information and may alert customers to additional needs. After evaluating the retailer's merchandise offering, customers may make a purchase or go to another retailer to collect more information. Eventually, customers make a purchase, use the product, and then decide whether the product satisfies their needs.

In some situations, customers spend considerable time and effort in selecting a retailer and evaluating the merchandise. In other situations, buying decisions are made automatically with little thought. There are mainly three types of customer decision making processes namely extended problem solving, limited problem solving and habitual decision making.

Extended Problem Solving

Extended Problem solving is a purchase decision process in which customers devote considerable time and effort to analyse alternatives. Customers typically engage in extended problem solving when the purchase decision involves a lot of risk and uncertainty. They are many types of risks. Financial risks arise when customers purchase an expensive product. Physical risks are important when customers feel a product may affect their health or safety. Social risks arise when customers believe a product will affect how others view them.

Customers engage in extended problem solving when they are making a buying decision to satisfy an important need or when they have little knowledge about the product or service. Due to high risk and uncertainty in these situations, customers go beyond their personal knowledge to consult with friends, family members, or experts. They may visit several retailers before making a purchase decision.

Retailers influence customers engaged in extended problem solving by providing the necessary information in a readily available and easily understood manner and by offering money-back guarantees. For example, retailers that sell merchandise involving extended problem solving provide brochures describing the merchandise and its specifications (for digital camera) have informational displays in the store (with CD, detail working and demo for household appliances like washing machine dishwasher); and use salespeople to make presentations and answer questions.

Limited Problem Solving

Limited Problem Solving is a purchase decision process involving a moderate amount of effort and time. Customers engage in this type of buying process when they have had some prior experience with the product or service and their risk is moderate. In these situations, customers tend to rely more on personal knowledge than on external information. They usually choose a retailer they have shopped at before and select merchandise they have bought in the past. Majority of customer decision making involves limited problem solving.

Retailers attempt to reinforce this buying pattern when customers are buying merchandise from them. If customers are shopping elsewhere, however, retailers need to break this buying pattern by introducing new information or offering different merchandise or services. One common type of limited problem solving is impulse buying. Impulse buying is a buying decision made by customers on the spot after seeing the merchandise.

Retailers encourage impulse buying behavior by using prominent displays to attract customer attention and stimulate a purchase decision based on little analysis. For example, sales of a grocery item are greatly increased when the item is featured in an end-aisle display, when a "BEST BUY" sign is placed on the shelf with the item, when the item is placed at eye level (typically on the third shelf from the bottom), or when items are placed at the checkout counter so customers can see them as they wait in line. Supermarkets use these displays and prime locations for the profitable items that customers tend to buy on impulse, such as gourmet food, rather than commodities such as flour and sugar, which are usually planned purchases. Impulse purchases by electronic shoppers are stimulated by putting special merchandise on the retailer's home page and by suggesting complementary merchandise.

Habitual Decision Making

Habitual Decision Making is a purchase decision process involving little or no conscious effort. Today's customers have many demands on their time. One way to cope with these time pressures is by simplifying their decision making process. When a need arises, customers may automatically respond with, "I'll buy the same thing I bought last time from the same store." Typically, this habitual decision making process is used when decisions aren't very important to customers and involve familiar merchandise they have bought in the past. Brand loyalty and store loyalty are examples of habitual decision making. Brand loyalty means that customers like and consistently buy a specific brand in a product category. They are reluctant to switch to other brands if their favorite isn't available. Thus, retailers can only satisfy these customers' needs if they offer the specific brands desired.

Store loyalty means that customers like and habitually visit the same store to purchase a type of merchandise. All retailers would like to increase their customers' store loyalty. Some approaches for increasing store loyalty are selecting a convenient location, offering complete assortments and reducing the number of stockouts, rewarding customers for frequent purchases, and providing good customer service.

THE BUYING PROCESS

Retailers try to influence the consumers as they go through the buying process and motivate them to buy the retailer's produce. When the need of the individual is recognized, he is becoming a potential customer. The various stages of buying process are;

1. Need Aroused

The buying process is triggered by the emergence of an unsatisfied need. An unsatisfied need arises, when the customer's current product does not meet his expectations or his stock is exhausted. The need motivating customers to go for shopping can be classified as functional needs and psychological needs. Functional needs are directly related to the performance of the product (*e.g.*) Fair and Lovely for fair face. Psychological needs are associated with personal gratification customers get from shopping, or owning the product. When purchased to satisfy psychological needs, the products functional characteristics are less important,(e.g.) purchasing a yellow colour designer saree. Functional needs are rational and psychological needs are emotional. Which need motivates the individual to act is important.

2. Recognition of the Need

Customers must recognize their unsatisfied need before they visit the store. Sometimes these needs are stimulated by an event. Advertising, direct mail, publicity and special events communicate the availability of merchandise or special price offer at the store. Within the store, visual display and salespeople can stimulate need recognition. Alternative window display can have dramatic impact on sales.

3. Level of Involvement

This is the amount of time and effort invested in the decision process. Involvement differs with complexity of product, the customer perceptions and the buying situation in which the purchase is to be made.

4. Information Search and Identification of Alternatives

Once customers identify the need, they seek information about retailers or product to satisfy the need. Brands come to mind immediately are referred to as **evoked set.** Friends, shop assistants, leaflets, magazine and advertisement provide a consideration set. The search for information occurs on an internal and external basis. Promotional campaign, new brand or product peer group influence will have major impact. Some customers who enjoy shopping will search for more, spend more time in store, assess the alternatives, and gather information from sales staff. If they do not get the required information, they may visit another retail store. More self confident customers search less. Besides, there are routine shoppers, who know in advance what they want and where to find it. Here the competitive brands and time pressure will influences the customer. Potential customer will continue to collect information until they are satisfied and their intended purchase is acceptable.

5. Evaluation of Alternatives

Comparisons are made by the potential purchaser based on his expected attributes like cost, reputation, performance expectation, *etc.* This is a complex stage. The customers will form some ranking preference among the alternatives. They try to balance and satisfy both functional and psychological needs. Usually the customer will form a purchase intention at this stage but they could seek additional information or delay the purchase.

6. Decision

Choice is made as part of a problem solving exercise to select on the basis of overall balance of evaluation. The most favoured offer, brand and method of purchase are selected.

7. Purchase Action

The purchase action may be affected by the available merchandise. (e.g.) colour, size, *etc.* The type of transaction, credit facilities and payment methods may also affect the purchase event. The steps to be taken by the retailer to convert the customers' positive product evaluations into actual purchase are,

- Do not stock out of popular merchandise
- Do not follow liberal return policies
- Offer credit
- Easy and quick checkout terminals
- Reduce the customer's waiting time

8. Post Purchase Behaviour

Quite often after the important purchase, the buyer will doubt the wisdom of their choice or have some dissatisfaction. He may have a need for reassurance. This arises when tension results from holding two conflicting ideas or beliefs at the same time. This psychological state of anxiety is reduced by means of guarantee, telephone helpline and detail advertisement. The post purchase process is related to how well the customers have been satisfied on the basis of their expectations of the product and store.

FACTORS AFFECTING CONSUMER DECISION MAKING

A consumer's purchase decision tends to be affected by the following four factors:

1. Demographic Factors

Demographic factors are unique to a particular person. They are objectives, quantifiable, and easily identifiable population data such as sex, income, age, marital status, *etc.* It also involves identification for who is responsible for the decision-making or buying and who is the ultimate consumer. In Tamilnadu, Saravana Stores and Shoppers' Stop, have focused themselves on respective segments based on demographic factors such as income, age, family size, gender, occupation, education, nature and number of vehicles owned, *etc.*

2. Psychological Factors

Psychological factors refer to the intrinsic or inner aspects of the individual. An understanding of consumers' psychology guides the marketers' segmentation strategy. For example, consumers respond differently towards the same retail marketing mix due to their respective motives, personality, perception, learning, level of involvement and attitude.

3. Environmental Factors

Environment denotes the surroundings which influence the consumer decision. The environmental factors influence consumers' wants, learning, motives, *etc.*, which in turn influence the shopping behaviour of the individual. Environmental factors cover all the physical and social characteristics of a consumer's external world, including physical objects (goods and outlets), spatial relationships (location of the shopping centre and merchandise in stores), and the social factors (opinion leaders, the person's family, co-customers, reference groups, social class, and culture).

The environment can be analysed at two levels – macro and micro. The macro environment includes large-scale, general environmental factors such as economic conditions with easy credit facility for durable goods and vehicles. Today, consumers in India are buying goods on easy instalments. There has been an increase in the population owning vehicles. This has made it viable to locate shopping centre out of city. The repeal of Land Ceiling Act and liberalisation and poor performance by stock markets has led to shift to funds towards trading and organised retail business. This has helped the Indian consumers to experience new kinds of formats with excellent and varied facilities.

These environmental drivers have a general influence on behaviour. The micro environment refers to the more tangible physical and social aspects of an individual's immediate surroundings. Examples of physical environment include aspects such as nature of the market structure, visual merchandise and display, roads and other infrastructural components. For instance, the congested lanes in the shopping centre and the transportation facility available are important aspects of the physical environment. Such factors have an immediate influence on consumers' buying and shopping behaviour. For example, consumers with cars normally avoid congested lanes.

4. Lifestyle Factors

Lifestyle refers to an individual mode of living. An individual's interests, opinion and activities influence his lifestyle. Lifestyle variables have been measured by identifying a consumer's day to day activities and interests. It is highly correlated with consumer's values and personality.

An individual's lifestyle is influenced by, the social group he belongs to and his occupation. For example, double-income-nucliear families in metros, shop very regularly at the super malls because of the limited time at their disposal, and they also look for entertainment while shopping on weekends. At the same time, they are higher spenders than, single-income families.

A study by imagesfashion.com highlights that Indian working women have to balance their wardrobe collection based on requirements of different occasions related to professional workplace or family gathering.

To cater to their specific requirements, different brands have emerged. In ethnic wear, there are just a handful of quality brands like Nalli, Kumarans, Bombay Selection, and Meena Bazaar. They have positioned themselves to meet the need for ethnic wear at family or festive occasions. On the otherhand, W(women store) and Khadder are trying to infuse global styling and design functionality with salwar kameez. It has created a women's career wear brand that is retailed in a smart, modern format that appeals to the lifestyle of their target segment.

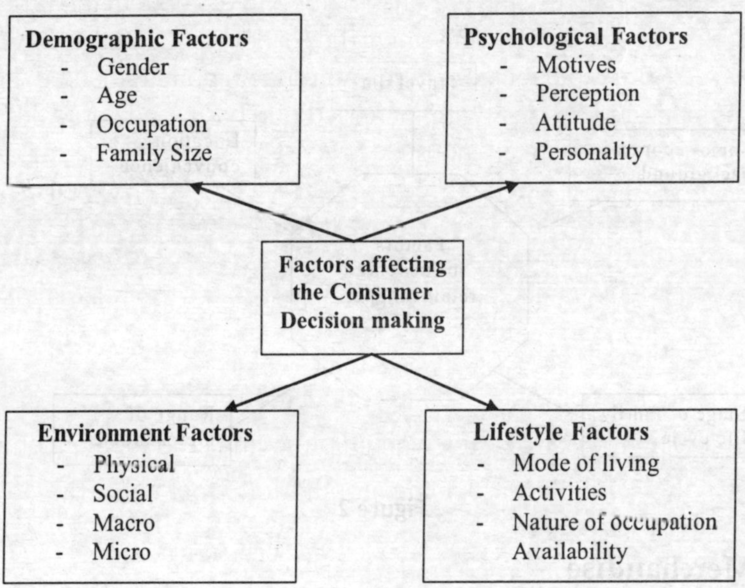

Figure 1

FACTORS INFLUENCING THE RETAIL SHOPPER

The behaviour of retail shoppers is a subject of study across the world. The basic difference however continues to be the maturity of markets and formats. While retail in the west has evolved in terms of formats over the past hundred years, organised retail in India is still a new phenomenon.

In India, retailers and retail formats are still evolving. Ten years ago, if a consumer wanted to buy soap, his only option was the local petty shop or the fair price shops run by the government. Today, he can still buy bar of soap from the same places, but he also has an option of going to a Food World, Big Bazaar, Food Land, an Apollo Pharmacy. Where will he buy? What are the reasons for his choosing one store over the other?

Understanding the reasons behind consumers choosing or patronising a store is important for the retailer. This is true for retailers across the world. In India, while new formats keep emerging, in many cases, the product offerings are similar.

The range available at the stores is also similar. Why should a customer visit a particular department store and not the company's own retail outlet? An insight into what provokes a customer to visit and patronise a store helps the retailer in strategy formulation.

The factors which influence the customer's decision making process are depicted in the following figure.

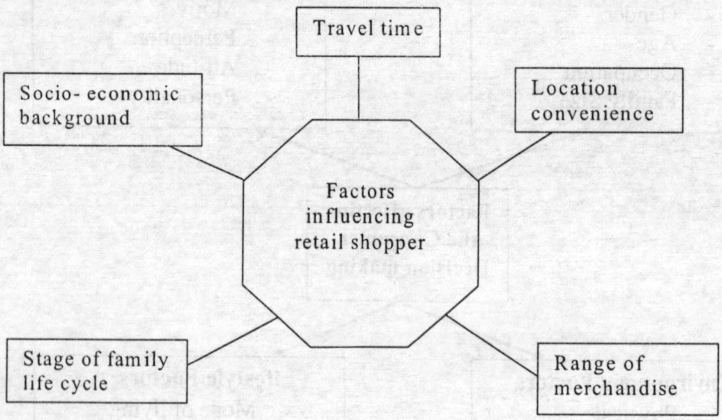

Figure 2

1. Range of Merchandise

The Range of Merchandise makes a customer to patronize a particular retail store. Initially curiosity may attract him to the retail store. But to retain him over a period of time, the quality and the range of merchandise offered by the store is essential.

2. Location Convenience

The element of convenience is fast gaining prominence in the world of organised retail. This is especially true in case of items like grocery\fruits and chemists. For example, while buying medicines, most patients would prefer to buy from the chemist near the doctor's clinic or near the hospital.

3. Travel Time

The time required to reach a particular retail location is again fast becoming critical. This is especially true in the case of metros like Mumbai, where travel time is high. This has resulted in many local areas developing in terms of shopping, to facilitate buying. We see the appearance of multiple outlets for a brand, departmental stores and malls making their appearance across most Indian cities.

4. Socio-economic Background

The socio-economic background of the consumer largely determines his lifestyle. This influences the kind of store that he may be comfortable shopping in. Consumer buying behaviour varies from market to market and is largely influenced by the culture of the region, for example, Asian culture is very different from Western culture. The need hierarchy is different for each market. The need that the retailer can fulfil needs to be clearly understood by him. It help him in determining the right merchandise mix and evolving an effective communication strategy. It is important for the retailer to consider the socio-economic changes in a region over a period of time which helps to understand the quality of life of the population and indirectly related to the spread of organised retailing.

5. Stage of Family Life Cycle

The Stage of the Family Life Cycle largely influence the customer needs. For example, the needs of a bachelor are different from the needs of the family man with children which again is different from the requirements of elderly couple. The retailer needs to be clear about his target market.

CUSTOMER SERVICE IN RETAILING

Customer service in retailing focuses on customer expectations. The ability of the retail organisation to identify these expectations and fulfill them will determine whether consumers enter the shop again and again. Service management, thus, aims to first measure customer expectations and then find ways of meeting them.

Customer service has two dimensions: the **services** and the **service**. While 'services' are the facilities, concessions or infrastructure offerings extended to customers; 'service' is how well they are offered by the store. For instance, in a garment store an alteration facility is part of the basket of services. If it is done well and the garment is delivered within the promised timeframe, then the service is said to be good. A retailer then needs to spell his service vision and create a service culture within the organisation. He has to set service standards with the right strategy, systems and people and manage processes and people to deliver them.

1. Defining the Service Objective

The first step to improving the quality of service is defining the objective for service performance in the organisation. A retailer needs to clearly decide upon service goals, and come up with the relevant strategies and systems. He has to understand the importance of service management to attain differentiated leadership in the industry, and thus, firm up his organisation's service objective. He also needs to give due importance to determining the profile of the store's customers, their expectations and the means to fulfill them.

2. Defining the Customer Profile and Expectations

Customer expectations often depend on the profile of the buyers catered to by the retail organisation. Good service means offering customers a little more than what they expect. For example, after eating in the restaurant of a five-star hotel, the customer expects the bill given to him to be placed in a leather folder. But in a non-graded restaurant, the bill can just be placed on the table. Hence, studying the profile of the customers and his expectations will enable retailers to design a complete service process.

Customer expectations can be broken up into:

Basic: Absolutely essential attributes of the experience.

Expected: Associated attributes of the experience that the customer takes for granted.

Desired: Attributes the customer doesn't expect, but knows about them and appreciates it if the experience includes them.

Unanticipated: 'Surprise' attributes that add value for the expectation.

3. Developing the Service Vision

The organisation's service vision emanates from its intent to serve its customers. The vision statement reflects what the management wants the store to become and be known for in terms of customer service. It can be called the 'defined future state of the business' in relation to the customer and the value he receives or would receive. The vision needs to be shared and communicated for uniform understanding and to enable the right delivery so that maximum customer satisfaction can be achieved.

4. Mapping the Processes

The customer service process starts with the customer expressing his need, and ends when it is fulfilled. To begin, the retailer has to decide on all the elements of the process to be implemented. He then has to compare them with the current processes and map them according to the desired status. The process ends with an operational plan after a careful review.

The following are the goals of the process:

Dependability: Does the service provider (Retailer) do what is promised?

Responsiveness: Is the service being provided in a timely manner?

Authority: Does the service provider create a feeling of confidence in the customer during the service delivery process?

Empathy: Is the service provider taking into account the customer's point of view?

Tangible Evidence: Is there evidence of the service being performed?

5. Setting Standards and Developing a Service Strategy

After identifying area of improvement and redesigning processes, it is necessary to now set new standards and design methods to make each department or function progressive, resulting in total customer focus. Take the example of a garment store that, affect process mapping, has found that it can increase customer satisfaction by reducing the delivery time of the altered garment from the current 24 hours to half-an-hour. It has to design its methods of functioning in such a way that each garment being altered is attended to on time, concentrating its resources on it and setting up the required infrastructure. The strategy is to use customer service to differentiate the retail organisation in the minds of the customers.

6. Managing and Developing Human Resources

Efficient customer service is all about putting people behind products and services. Human resources need to be trained at all levels to deliver the most efficient customer service as it is they who make the moments 'magical' for the customers. Further it is the store personnel who are the 'face' of the organisation to the customers. Communicating the organisation's vision, values, plans and strategies to the employees work wonders. They can then deliver excellent customer service to achieve the organisation's service vision. Developing an effective training and development plan for the whole organisation also helps people to operate a lot more efficiently.

7. Monitoring, Measuring and Filling Gaps in Service Quality

The retailer needs to monitor quality of service to ensure that service goals are being met, that service strategies are successful, and to find out how well the systems are supporting the process. Monitoring service quality means the continuous measurement of service quality parameters and evaluating them. The reason for measuring something is to understand it so that it can be done better or differently. From the angle of service quality, this means either identifying an opportunity for improvement, establishing a baseline for improvement, or verifying that the task has been accomplished.

Retailers who really believe that service quality is important for their success appreciate the need for continuous measurement of all service parameters. Monitoring and measurement can be considered a way to close the loop around the service quality improvement effort, to lead and guide rather than drive it. The measurements help everybody know how well they are accomplishing what they have to do. Service quality measurement being a continuous process, the retailer needs to clearly state the value he would like to deliver to his customers; all the aspects of service quality need to be understood by every employee. They should be well-trained on how to deliver value to the customer. Every employee must be made to understand the organisation's service vision and objectives.

Some retailers use 'mystery shoppers' to evaluate the service quality performance. Since quality of service is a subjective assessment, each person values is based on his own expectations and perceptions. If not clearly briefed on the parameters on which they need to evaluate service, the finding of the mystery shoppers may not be too accurate.

8. Service Qualities to be Measured

The objective of every service quality monitoring and measuring exercise is to primarily evaluate customer satisfaction levels. But before a retailer actually starts measuring it based on customer feedback he needs to do an organizational assessment of the service and culture of the organisation by considering the following:

Value delivered to the customer.

- The internal effectiveness of the organisation, and areas in need of improvement.
- Quality of work life, as it has a bearing on how efficiently they work.
- The need for a service quality initiative to achieve the desired quality standards.
- The chances of the service quality initiative succeeding in the organisation.
- Top management's commitment to the effort and its capability to ensure that it does succeed.

Most retailers measure service quality performance only at the store level.

To be a truly service-oriented organisation, the retailer needs to monitor and measure service quality of all departments/functions, both at the front and back ends. The entire organisation should be one big customer service department, where everybody is responsible for service quality. Every department and employee should be accountable to the other and all departments/functions need to be given the same level of importance.

Once service quality performance has been monitored and measured internally, the results need to be carefully studied and analysed. Based on this analysis, appropriate feedback has to be given to the employees and corrective actions taken in right earnest. After measuring the culture and service quality performance internally, the retailer can consider soliciting customer feedback.

9. Implementation after Monitoring and Measuring Service Quality

The key factor in closing the loop is not measurement but the information itself, in the hands of those who best respond and act on it. The right dissemination of the information and results of the measurement is critical to enhance service quality performance.The entire process of monitoring and measuring service quality has to be regarded as a feedback mechanism rather than as a controlling tool.

The retailer needs to create a feedback mechanism that communicates to the employees as to how the organisation in general and they in particular are faring on service quality and reengineer processes to fill the gaps.

Service quality is a continuous process and involves every employee in the organisation. Monitoring and measuring service quality performance provides the organisation and its employees a live scoreboard to know how they are faring. A retailer's commitment to this process – and the resulting action that goes into creating and using this process wisely – will help to make service quality a differentiator for the organisation and ensure that it emerges a winner.

CUSTOMER PROFILING

A customer profile is a series of descriptive phrases that paint a picture of a selected retail consumer target. A good profile will answer the questions

"Who are these people?" and "Where do they live?"

A profile is built from demographic, expenditure, lifestyle and media preference data and is used to immediately understand the characteristics of a given customer. Profiling is an effective tool because it helps retail marketers manage current customers, develop strategies aimed at specific prospects and reduce the overall costs of marketing and customer acquisition.

Using profiles to explore untapped markets is one of the most effective ways to increase retail direct marketing response rates and ultimately acquire new customers. A good profile leverages known demographic, expenditure and behavioral characteristics against an unknown population and reveals similarities or differences you can exploit.

MARKET SEGMENTATION

Retail Marketers and analysts use segmentation to organize and manage market and customer data. A segment is built by analyzing data and grouping (clustering) elements that share sought characteristics (in the case of retail, demographic, expenditure, lifestyle and media preference information). Segmentation is essential for cost effective, accurately targeted direct marketing. By organizing customer and market data in this way, organizations are able to understand the differences and similarities between groups of customers and prospects, and develop effective messaging, products and distribution channels appropriate to the specific needs and wants of a given segment.

Market Segmentation is the process of dividing the heterogeneous total market into small groups of customers who share a similar set of wants. Each of these smaller groups possesses somewhat homogenous characteristics. As in case of marketers in other businesses, marketers in the business of retailing may also seek the benefits of market segmentation depending on his unique market and business context. For example, a retailer may divide women customers into two segments: working women and housewife, if he finds that these two groups have different sets of needs.

A segment is a relatively homogenous group and hence, responds to a marketing mix in a similar way. Different groups or segments require different promotional strategies and marketing mixes because they have different wants and needs. A niche is a more narrowly defined group seeking a distinctive mix of benefits. Marketers usually identify niches by dividing a segment into sub-segments. For example, the retailer may divide the segment of working women into two sub-segments, those with children and those without children.

Segmentation helps the retailer to customize the product/service and tailor its promotional campaigns. This helps the retailer to reach out to meet the specific needs of a narrowly defined customer group. Segmentation of markets is imperative and often crucial to the development of effective marketing programmes in today's competitive marketplace. The obstacle for market segmentation is heterogeneous customer needs and shopping behavior/patterns, which no single retailer is in a position to serve as per their desired level of needs.

The Benefits of Market Segmentation

Retailers segment the market to identify specific groups of customers in their trade area on whom their selling efforts can be concentrated. Such focused selling efforts are aimed at making the retailer the preferred destination for such identified segments for the products or services it deals in and to develop a dominant position in the target segments. Following are the benefits of segmenting the market.

(a) Understand Customer Behaviour

Segmentation helps a retailer to gain insight into why the target group acts the way it does. The buying behaviour of the target segment can be understood once the market is segmented. This can help in the development of an effective marketing strategy.

(b) Positioning

Segmentation helps a retailer in positioning itself in the market. Thus, Shoppers' Stop and Crossroads have targeted the upper income class while Westside has targeted the larger base of middle and upper middle-class consumers.

(c) Development of Marketing Mix

Segmentation helps a retailer in identifying the target population and developing a customised marketing programme in terms of product/service offering, price strategy and promotional programme.

(d) Promotional Campaigns

Segmentation helps a retailer in developing more effective and accurate promotional campaigns.

(e) Merchandising Decisions

Segmentation helps a retailer in merchandising decisions. Merchandising is essentially the skill that decides which items will go on the shelves. An understanding of preferences of target segments is essential for a successful merchandising programme.

(f) Store Location Decision

Segmentation helps a retail chain in deciding locations for its new stores. The retail outlets can be located where there is a concentration of the target population.

SEGMENTING RETAIL MARKETS

No one approach is best for all retailers. They must explore various factors that affect customer buying behaviour and determine which factors are most important.

1. Geographic Segmentation

Geographic Segmentation groups customers by where they live. A retail market can be segmented by countries like Japan, India, Mexico, *etc.*, and by areas within a country such as states, cities and neighbourhoods. Since customers typically shop at stores convenient to where they live and work, individual retail outlets usually focus on the customer segment reasonably close to the outlet. In India, many food retailers concentrate on a particular region or state of the country. Even within a State, stores in a chain must adjust to unique needs of customers in different neighbourhoods. For example, supermarkets in Tier I city typically have more branded, packed ready to use foods than stores in Tier II city.

Segments based on geography are identifiable, accessible and substantial. It's easy to determine who lives in a geographic segment such as the Chennai metropolitan area and to target communications and locate retail outlets for customers in Chennai. When customers in different geographic segments have similar needs, it would be inappropriate to develop unique retail offerings by geographic markets. For example, a grocery customer in Chennai probably seeks the same benefits as a grocery customer in Coimbatore. Thus, it wouldn't be useful to segment the grocery market geographically. Even though Target and the Gap vary some merchandise assortments geographically, the majority of their merchandise is identical in all of their stores because customers who buy basic groceries have the same needs in all regions of the TamilNadu State.

2. Demographic Segmentation

Demographic Segmentation groups consumers on the basis of easily measured, objective characteristics such as age, gender, income and education. Demographic variables are the most common means to define segments because consumers in these segments can be easily identified and accessed. The media used by retailers to communicate with customers are defined in terms of demographic profiles. Demographics such as gender are related to differences in shopping behaviour. Men show little ability or interest in improving their shopping skills, whereas women view the supermarket as a place where thy can demonstrate their expertise in getting the most value for their money. Rather than looking for items on sale or making price comparisons, men tend to select well-known brands. They also tend to not pay attention at the checkout register, whereas women watch the cashier to be sure they're charged the right price. Men and women even buy different merchandise. Women buy more health-oriented foods like pulses and refrigerated butter and household essentials such as cleaning and personal health products. Men's shopping baskets contains more beverages, cupcakes and ice cream. Men also do less planning and make numerous last-minute grocery trips. These eleventh-hour trips make men more susceptible to impulse purchases such as potato chips and soft drinks.

However, demographics may not be useful for defining segments for some retailers. For example, demographics are poor predictors of users of active wear such as jogging suits and running shoes. At one time, retailers assumed that active wear would be purchased exclusively by young people, but the health and fitness trend has led people of all ages to buy this merchandise. Relatively inactive consumers find active wear to be comfortable. Initially, retailers felt that VCRs would be a luxury product purchased mainly by wealthy customers. But retailers found that low-income customers and families with young children were strongly attracted to VCRs because they offered low-cost, convenient entertainment.

3. Geodemographic Segmentation

Geodemographic Segmentation uses both geographic and demographic characteristics to classify customers. This segmentation scheme is based on the principle that "birds of feather flock together". Consumers in the same neighbourhoods tend to buy the same types of cars, appliances and apparel and shop at the same types of retailers. The most widely used tool for geodemographic segmentation is PRIZM (Potential Rating Index by Zip Market) developed by Claritas in USA. Claritas identified 62 geodemographic segments, called neighbourhoods or clusters, by using detailed demographic and consumption information and data on media habits of the people. Geodemographic Segmentation is particularly appealing to store-based retailers, because customers typically patronize stores close to their neighbourhood. Thus, retailers can use geodemographic segmentation to select locations for their stores and tailor assortment in the stores to the preferences of the local community.

4. Lifestyle Segmentation

Lifestyle or psychographics refers to how people live, how they spend their time and money, what activities they pursue and their attitudes and opinions about the world in which they live. The segments are identified through consumer surveys. Retailers today are placing more emphasis on lifestyles than on demographics to define a target segment. Lifestyle segmentation are described by two dimensions.

(i) The customers' resources, including their income, education, health, and energy level, and

(ii) Personal orientation or what motivates them – principles, status, or actions. Principle-oriented consumers are guided by their internal values rather than the opinions of others. Status-oriented consumers strive to win the approval of others. Action-oriented people seek activity, variety, and risk in their daily lives.

In USA, Nature's Northwest focuses on a lifestyle segment of consumers interested in health and wellness. The 42,000 square-foot Nature's Northwest combines an upscale supermarket and natural-foods store with unexpected offerings such as fitness classes and spa/ salon services. Shoppers can take a yoga class, soak in a hydrotherapy tub, learn about herb gardening, or get their hair coloured. An on-site interactive learning centre and lending library is devoted to health and related subjects. The pharmacy offers conventional therapies as well as homeopathic remedies.

Lifestyle segmentation is useful because it identifies what motivates buying behaviour. On the other hand, it is difficult to identify and access consumers in specific lifestyle segments.

5. Buying Situation Segmentation

Buying behaviour of customers with the same demographics or lifestyle can differ depending on their buying situation. Thus, retailers may use buying situations such as fill-in versus weekly shopping to segment a market.

6. Benefit Segmentation

Another approach for defining a target segment is to group customers seeking similar benefits, this is called benefit segmentation. For example, customers who place high importance on fashion and style and low importance on price would form a fashion segment, whereas customers who place more importance on price would form a price segment. Benefits segments are very actionable. Benefits sought by customers in the target segment clearly indicate how retailers should design their offerings to appeal to the segment. But customers in benefit segments aren't easily identified or accessed. It's hard to look at a person and determine what benefits he or she is seeking.

7. Custom Segmentation

DMS Retail can deliver customized segmentation systems to Retail clients based on their specific requirements and circumstances. A custom segmentation system blends client data with DMS Retail's detailed consumer information databases to build actionable consumer and market intelligence, inform strategic messaging or positioning and refine targets. Often a retailer will require a custom segmentation system to support a large, data-centric initiative or to organize and leverage under utilized data assets. DMS Retail's ability to produce comprehensive segmentation systems at the most granular level gives retailers a competitive advantage in the marketplace.

8. Predictive Segmentation

Predictive segmentation embeds a predictive element into each of retailer's segments, so not only do the consumers in each segment look and act alike today, they will look and act alike in the future. In this way, the predictive element helps to define the segment. The key benefit to retail marketers is, it is a tool that can be used today and in the future. In addition, the predictive scores can be used independently to support tactical initiatives. For example, if we are building a retention model we can add the predictive scores; this will allow us to see which customers show the greatest likelihood to attrite in the short and long term.

9. Composite Segmentation Approaches

No one approach meets all the criteria for useful customer segmentation. For example, segmenting by demographics and geography is ideal for identifying and accessing customers, but these characteristics often are unrelated to customers' needs. Thus, these approaches may not indicate the actions necessary to attract customers in these segments. On the other hand, knowing what benefits customers are seeking is useful for designing an effective retail offering, the problem is identifying which customers are seeking these benefits. For these reasons, composite segmentation plans use multiple variables to identify customers in the target segment. They define target customers by benefits sought, lifestyles and demographics. Targeting allows a retail enterprise to channel its marketing budget where there is the greatest and fastest possibility of Return On Investment (ROI).

In terms of overall business strategy, retailer's ability to identify and understand consumers helps them to make accurate estimates about the potential for their products and services in a given market, as well as support and direct merchandise development strategies to both new and existing customers. Whether retailer's target is current customers or new prospects, in markets known or unknown, an effective targeting model reduces the risk of any new venture.

Blending Demographic, Behavioural, Expenditure and Media Preference data with retailer-specific data and applying data mining technologies outperform all other direct marketing techniques. In addition, methodology that should be used must be dynamic to allow the sights to be reset frequently to keep targets in focus consistently.

MAIN THEORIES OF CONSUMER BEHAVIOUR

The discipline of consumer behaviour has borrowed many concepts from the quantitative and behavioural sciences to generate integrated models of action.

Models of behaviour are a useful means of organizing disparate bodies of knowledge regarding social action into a somewhat arbitrary yet plausible process of intervening psychological, social, economic and behavioural variables.

These models share several common points:

1. They all exhibit consumer behaviour as a decision process.
2. They provide a comprehensive model focusing mainly on the behaviour of the individual consumer.
3. They share the belief that behaviour is rational and hence can, in principle, be explained.
4. They view buying behaviour as purposive, with the consumers as an active information seeker.
5. They believe that consumers limit the amount of information taken in, and more over time from general notions to more specific criteria and preference of alternatives
6. They all include a notion of feedback – that is, outcomes from purchases will affect future purchases.

A brief overview of some models will provide a better understanding of the decision making process.

ENGEL-KOLLAT-BLACKWELL (EKB) MODEL

Engel-Kollat-Blackwell (EKB) Model has been widely referenced and is acknowledged as one of the most comprehensive explanations of consumer behaviour. The original model has undergone three major revisions since 1968 and the current model, while retaining some of the fundamentals, has become more sophisticated in definitional and explanatory aspects and therefore varies form the original version. This reflects the progress made in knowledge which required some adaptation to the original model for its continued survival.

The EKB model takes a broad view, incorporating inputs such as perception and learning which are discussed in great detail. A key feature of the EKB model is its incorporation of the differences between high and low involvement as part of the buying process. High involvement is normally present in the decision-making process when the perceived risk in the purchase is high. This element of risk is higher when the consumer is unsure about the outcome of his or her purchase decision.

This arises when:

(1) Information is limited

(2) The buyer has low confidence

(3) The price is high

The EKB model has the decision process as pathways of convergence passing through various stages of processing prior to any choice being made. The central process can be seen to incorporate five stages:

(1) Problem recognition/arousal

(2) Internal search – alternative evaluation

(3) External search – alternative evaluation

(4) Choice/purchase

(5) Outcomes as dissonance or satisfaction

The environmental factors, such as cultural norms and values, motives, etc., which influence these stages are important. The model incorporates influence which moves from the general to specific, which is from the macro level(reference group, social class, norms) to the micro level (belief, intention, attitude).

SHETH'S FAMILY MODEL OF BEHAVIOUR

Quite often the purchase decision process is investigated in terms of the individual; for example, some models have stressed the individual as the single focus of attention. It is clear that for the purchase of high price items the decision process involves a high level of risk that the decision may be a poor one. It also often involves the preference resolution of more than one individual. This creates a complex situation whereby, the purchase has to satisfy the divergent needs of the group. Obviously a family decision involves multiple influences form its members. Within the theory of family buying behaviour there is the concept of role structure, that is, individual members of the family take on roles such as collecting information, deciding on the available budgets, etc. Whatever way a family makes its final decisions we have to realise we are not dealing with a homogeneous unit but with a collection of individuals with difference goals, needs, motives and interests.

The Sheth model of the family decision process provides one of the few examples of an attempt to replicate the behavioural of group decision making. The problem with the model is that aspects of search, motives, beliefs and predispositions occur in tandem with each member of the group prior to there being a resolution of the group to a final decision, whereby joint or autonomous outcomes occur. While we have to applaud Sheth for breaking away from an overreliance by theorists on individual decision models, we may need to question the reality of his model as to how groups bargain and trade-off parts of the larger decision, especially in relation to products shared by members of the family.

Though the above model shows the individual and group influence in the choice of product and the retail store, a customer select a particular retail shop depending upon the following points,

1. general store characteristics (reputation, number of stores);
2. physical characteristics of the store (decor, cleanliness, checkout services);
3. convenience of reaching the store from the consumer's location (time, parking, etc.);
4. products offered (variety, dependability, quality);
5. prices charged by the store (value, special sales);
6. store personnel (courteous, friendly, helpful);
7. advertising by the store (informative, believable, appealing); and,
8. friends' perception of the store (well known, liked, recommended).

To conclude, the retail sector has specific skill shortages in Sales skills, Product knowledge, Customer communication, Customer service, Small business management, Food handling and hygiene and Work place training and supervision .The retail industry employs more people than any other industry sector and has a unique age profile-more youngsters between the age 15 to 24 in retailing. It is one of the fastest growing industry nationally. n the long run interest,to satisfy the dynamic customer needs, today's retail marketing managers must:

- Understand the connections between the lifestyle and expenditure characteristics of customers, their propensity to purchase one product or brand over another, and leverage this understanding for competitive advantage.
- Improve direct marketing response by ensuring the retailers are targeting the right households at the right time, using the right media with the right message.
- Leverage current consumer data to make better strategic decisions about products, marketing and locations.
- Increase customer loyalty and retention with a scientific, data driven approach to analytical CRM.
- Applying advanced analytics to current demographic, expenditure and lifestyle data produces the most accurate customer segments and profiles. With a clear picture of different customer segments, retailers are in a position to develop merchandise and offer that meet the needs of existing customers and answer the needs of targeted prospects.

Questions

I. Fill in the Blanks

1. Understanding ____________ needs help the retailer to place the right product in the hands of the consumer.
2. The buying process begins when the customer recognize his ________ need.
3. ______________ is a purchase decision process in which customers devote considerable time to analyse alternatives.
4. __________ buying is a buying decision made by customers on the spot.
5. Brands immediately come to mind are referred to as __________.

Answers

1. consumer 2. unsatisfied 3. Extended problem solving 4. Impulse 5. Evoked set

II. Choose the Best Answer

1. __________ decision making is used when familiar merchandise is bought by consumer.

   (a) Habital (b) Impulse (c) On the spot (d) Careful

2. __________ customers search less for their product.

   (a) Emotional (b) Self confident (c) Knowledgeable (d) Educated

3. Population data such as sex, income, age are __________ factors.

   (a) Cultural (b) Social (c) Demographic (d) Lifestyle

4. Continuous measurement of service quality parameters in retail shop is known as __________ service quality.

   (a) measuring (b) filling (c) monitoring (d) gap-filling

5. A __________ profile is series of descriptive phases that give selected retail consumer target.

   (a) seller (b) buyer (c) middlemen (d) customer

Answers

1. a 2.b 3.c 4. c 5. d

III. Answer in One Word

1. Define Market Segmentation
2. What is habital decision making?
3. Mention the four factor that influence consumer decision making.
4. What is Composite Segmentation?
5. Mention the two main theories of consumer behaviour.

IV. Essay Questions

1. What are the common points shared by the theories of consumer behaviour. Discuss EBK Model in detail.
2. Explain market segmentation. What are the benefits of segmentation?
3. Explain various approaches to segment retail markets.
4. Discuss the various steps to render better service to retail customer.
5. Explain the demographic, psychological, environmental and lifestyle factors that influence consumer decision making.
6. Discuss the factors influencing retail shopper.
7. Explain the steps in buying process.

Chapter 3
RETAIL MERCHANDISING

INTRODUCTION

The success of any retail operation is based on the retailer's ability to provide the right goods to the consumer, at the right place, at the right time and at the right price. The entire process of procuring a product/service needed by the consumer and ensuring that it reaches the place where consumer can conveniently buy it is integral to the success of any retail store. The process of merchandising covers all the functions involved in identifying the right product for the retailer, sourcing it and ensures that it reaches the end consumer. The term merchandising is unique and exclusive to the retail industry. It refers to the entire process of inventory planning and management in a retail organization. Merchandising can be termed as the planning, buying and the selling of merchandise. The merchandising is an integral part of retailing and one of the most challenging functions of retailer. Merchandising, when done properly, leads to an increase in Return On Investment (ROI). The greater the ROI, the higher the profitability. Hence for a retailer, the objective of merchandise planning is to achieve the following seven rights:

- Right Product
- Right Place
- Right quantity
- Right Price
- Right Mix
- Right time

The function of merchandising is to achieve all these rights, so that sales are high with an ideal level of inventory holding and thus more profits.

Merchandising or merchandise management can be termed as the analysis, planning, acquisition, handling and control of the merchandise and investments in a retail organisation.

- Analysis to identify their customers by retailers.

- Planning because what is procured now is to be sold in the future to ultimate consumers.
- Control is essential since merchandising needs huge investment. Such financial investment to ensure adequate return should be properly monitored and controlled.

Merchandising is the day-to-day business of all retailers. As inventory is sold, new stocks to be purchased displayed and sold. Hence, merchandising is considered as core of retailing. Merchandising does not function in isolation. It is affected by various factors like the organisation structure, the size of the retail organisation, types of stores and merchandise to be carried.

MERCHANDISE HIERARCHY

While planning the merchandise mix, a retail organisation has to start with a clear definition of its merchandise hierarchy. The merchandise hierarchy is a disciplined way of grouping the merchandise mix at different levels, starting from a high-level grouping to the lowest level of the stock-keeping unit (SKU). The grouping may at times have even more than four-five levels as shown in the following example.(See Fig.1).

The merchandise hierarchy forms the platform needed to create the store's merchandise mix. The merchandising vision for the store dictates the different divisions and the lower rungs that the store must have in the hierarchy.

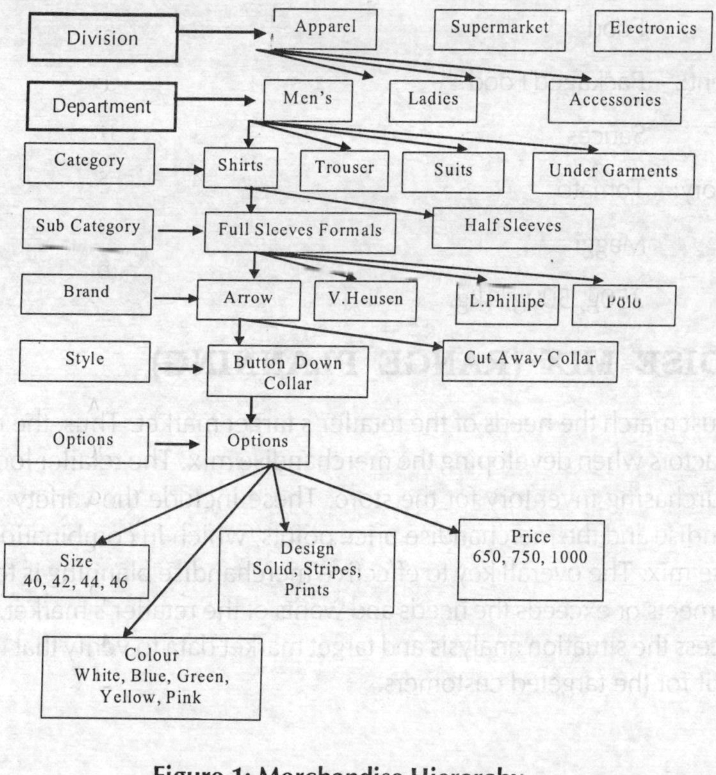

Figure 1: Merchandise Hierarchy

Building the stores merchandise mix by following concept of merchandise hierarchy has it advantages:

(a) One can define in terms of ratios the mix of elements at each level of the hierarchy.

(b) One can analyse and drill down through the rungs of the hierarchy to the problem areas, if any, up to SKU level.

(c) One can remove or add elements following security escalations. This means if the store's merchandise decisions have to be taken based on the performance, say, of the millions of SKUs contributing to the formation of the merchandise pyramid for the store–the peak being the divisions – decisions at the lower rungs can be taken by front-line personnel. Those at the higher levels, which would impact the merchandise proposition/image of the store, can be taken by the higher-ups.

SKU

To use the example (see Fig.1), a 40-size white shirt of solid design at the price-point of ` 750 having a button-down collar of the Arrow brand in the full sleeves sub-category or sub-class of the shirts category belonging to the men's department of the apparel division in a retail organisation is an SKU. The levels in the merchandise hierarchy may be different for various product categories. For instance, in a supermarket, the levels may be:

Division:	Food
Department:	Packaged Food
Category:	Sauces
Sub-category:	Tomato
Brand:	Maggi
Options:	250g, 500g, 1kg.

MERCHANDISE MIX (RANGE PLANNING)

Inventory must match the needs of the retailer's target market. Thus, the retailer needs to consider several factors when developing the merchandise mix. The retailer looks for a number of things when purchasing inventory for the store. These include the variety, assortment and quality of merchandise and the merchandise price points, which in combination are referred to as the merchandise mix. The overall key to effective merchandise planning is to ensure that the merchandise mix meets or exceeds the needs and wants of the retailer's market. Once again the retailer should access the situation analysis and target market data to verify that the merchandise is indeed a good fit for the targeted customers.

1. Variety

The number of product lines (or categories) the retailer stocks is referred to as the variety, or breadth. Breadth can also refer to the number of brands carried within a product line. For example, shoe retailers need to decide whether to carry just athletic shoes, work shoes and boots or to offer a wider variety of products including dress shoes. They also must decide whether to carry a limited assortment of shoe accessories or a full line of shoe accessories.

Breadth is often described along a continuum of narrow or broad. A store that offers twenty lines of shoes may be said to have broad variety (breadth).

In contrast, a store that offers only one line may be said to offer a narrow variety (breadth).

The merchandise variety must be consistent with the retailer's mission and should be developed with the retailer's objectives in mind. The customer will make a number of decisions about the retailer based on the merchandise mix.

2. Assortment

Merchandise assortment or depth, consists of the stock-keeping units (SKU) within a category (this could include types of brands, colours and sizes that the retailer stocks within each line it carries). Depth is often described along a continuum of shallow to deep.

Merchandise depth is directly related to quality, assortment and variety of merchandise offered. To monitor merchandise depth, retailers use stock-keeping units (SKUs), to determine the average quantity of merchandise carried for each of the various brands sold in their stores. An SKU is the smallest unit of measure used to inventory products. SKUs are established by the retailer and are typically an alphanumeric combination. For example, a shirt of a particular style and colour could have an SKU of 012512-A, meaning 'style number 012512, in Yellow'. An SKU tells the retailer exactly what product is in inventory. The SKU may or may not be visible to the customer.

The retailer must let the buyer know the assortment policy so that the buyer can develop a merchandise mix that is in line with the retailer's mission, vision and objectives.

One problem retailer's face when developing their merchandise assortment is achieving an appropriate balance between their own brands (private labels) and the national assortment of products (national brands). This balance is important because the retailer has to allocate shelf space for each of these products. National brands generally have a smaller profit margin for the retailer but are supported with national advertising. Thus, there is consumer demand for these products. In contrast, private labels provide higher margins but carrying them also requires communicating the brands to consumers and developing consumer brand loyalty to the private labels. Currently, private label brands are growing at a faster rate than national brands.

3. Quality

Suppliers of merchandise provide varying levels of quality in their merchandise assortments. Therefore, retailers must decide what levels of quality they want when purchasing inventory. Consumers have developed firm attitudes and opinions regarding the quality of products. Thus, the retailer needs to be clear about what its consumers want from a product (long life, low price, and so on) and to offer the appropriate merchandise mix of high-quality and/or lower-quality products.

Once again the retailer should look to the retail mission and vision to determine what to offer the consumer in terms of quality. The merchandise quality should be consistent with all other messages communicated to the consumer about the retail operation. A retailer that is located in an upscale area, uses high-quality communication vehicles, and offers an elegant shopping atmosphere complete with top-notch customer service should carry only high-quality merchandise. Conversely, a discount retailer's customers look primarily for value for their money. Therefore, the discount retailer should concentrate on merchandise that can be offered at a lower price. As a result, the overall merchandise mix should contain lower-quality products.

4. Price Points

Price points are another consideration when selecting merchandise assortments. Price points are the range of prices for a particular merchandise line. Price points help to attract the retailer's target market into the store. Retailers must decide if they want to have market-average, above-average, or below-average price points for the products they offer. Price points generally have a fairly wide range. The benefit of establishing price points early in the merchandise mix development process is that it helps the retailer select the market for the product. Consumers who are not interested in expensive, high-quality shoes will probably not be attracted to a shoe store that markets Z-Coils.

VARIABLES THAT AFFECT THE MERCHANDISE MIX: (OPTIMAL MERCHANDISE MIX)

Consumers need change, manufacturers develop new products and progressive retailers are continuously adding new products and dropping old ones. The merchandise mix not only satisfies the customer's wants but also shapes those wants and influences the consumer's buying decision. Therefore optimal merchandise mix depends on the trading area, retail format, scale of operation and the segment of market the store is serving. There are four constraining factors that influence the design of the optimal merchandise mix. They are budget constraints, space limitation product turnover and stock replenishment.

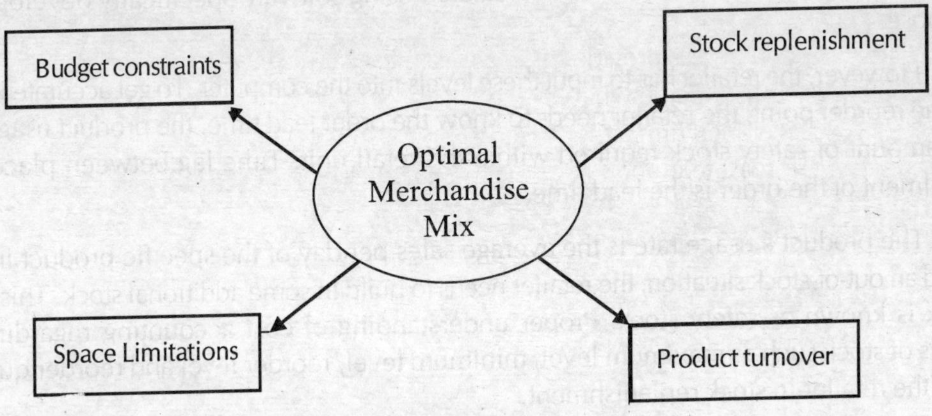

Figure 2

In creating the merchandise mix, a number of variables have an impact on merchandise purchases. These variables can hinder the retailer's ability to achieve merchandise mix goals and objectives. The main variables are budget constraints, space limitations, product turnover rate, and stock replenishment.

1. Budget Constraints

One problem encountered by many firms is that the retail buyer is constrained by the amount of money available to make purchases. The retail buyer must make the best decisions possible given a limited budget.

2. Space Limitations

Another problem is that the retailer's selling venue (store, catalogue, etc.) has inherent space limitations. Thus, the retailer has to decide which products will appeal most to consumers and at the same time return a good investment to the owners of the retail outlet.

3. Product Turnover Rates

Closely related to the problems of budget and storage limitations are product turnover rates. The more variety of merchandise a retailer carries (in other words, the greater the depth), the lower the turnover rate for all products. Although some products turn over faster than others, many retailers need to carry a lot of depth to ensure customer satisfaction. In addition, carrying too few units of a product may lead to a shortage situation.

4. Stock Replenishment

Finally, the retailer needs to know when the various levels of stock for the stores must be replenished. By establishing these stock levels, the retailer will known when to reorder the various products. Reorder points are calculated using software specifically developed for that purpose.

However, the retailer has to input these levels into the computer. To get accurate information on the reorder point, the retailer needs to know the order lead time, the product usage rate, and the amount of safety stock required within the retail unit. Time lag between placement and fulfillment of the order is the lead time.

The product's usage rate is the average sales per day of the specific product in units. To avoid an out-of-stock situation, the retailer needs to build in some additional stock. This additional stock is known as safety stock. Proper understanding of cost accounting regarding various levels of stock such as maximum level, minimum level, reorder level and reorder quantity will help the retailer in stock replenishment.

∴ Thus, the development of optimal merchandise mix requires:

- Understanding the selection process of consumers
- Deciding upon core and seasonal merchandise
- Agreeing the range – e.g., style, size and colour mix – depth and width
- Taking into consideration the sales-to-stock level targets and calculating the optimum level of stock by utilising one of the stock inventory planning methods.
- Relating the range plans to individual stores and possible promotional plans.
- Briefing the buyers on agreed source.

PLANOGRAM

There is another type of assortment plan that is emerging now. A graphical range plan is called the planogram. This sort of plan moves away from the purely numerical type of planning that has been used until now and allows the range to be put together in a visual way. Typically digitally stored images are manipulated into collage-type storyboards. Space planning software packages like that of AC Nielsen support such graphic base stock mapping, which helps in easy replenishment planning and effective store space utilization. Thus merchandise assortment planning and base stock mapping-numerical and visual-numerical methods respectively – enable one to take account of the space utilization in a store by calculating the Return and Space Employed or Returns on Footage.

CATEGORISING

A category is defined as a distinct manageable group of products that consumers perceive to be related and substitutable in meeting their needs and wants.

The complexity of modern retail operations requires the grouping of the buying process into an individual category. A category is a merchandise group that addresses similar consumer needs and wants. A category is an assortment of items which the consumer may perceive as substitute for each other. Goods in a category are displayed and sold together in a retail shop, so that customer choices are easier. It is pointed out that 75% of consumer brand decisions are made in front of the fixture and often within three seconds. Therefore, the category offering has to be managed to maximize sales and profits for the retailer and want satisfaction for the consumer.

CATEGORY MANAGEMENT

Category Management is the process by which a retail business is managed with the objective of maximizing the sales and profits of a category. It indicates that retailers will organise their merchandising activities around brands so as to maximize sales and profit. Category management approach calls for category manager who is taking the total responsibility of that one category. The success or failures of a category will ultimately the responsibility of the category manager. It leads to ideal combination of sizes and vendors which will earn more profit from the allocated space.

Retailers and vendors sharing information about the customers served by them will help to manage the inventories in a better way. At times, retailers may have a favoured vendor known as category captain who will supply readily to satisfy customer needs and improve the performance and profit potential, for the entire category.

Category management is the current approach to assortment decision-making. It adopts an explicit customer perspective and takes a holistic view of product groups. For a given category of products, the merchandising policy has to meet the range needs of the target customer without unnecessary duplication. Two similar products alongside each other on the shelf are likely to impact on each other's rate of stock-turn. From the retailer's perspective, it may not be worthwhile to be stocking both. In consequence each individual product line has to justify its place in the range in terms of meeting customer needs. However, it may result in conflict between retailer and supplier.

Category management would be relatively straightforward if sales volumes remained constant overtime, but they are not so. Retailers need to plan fulfillment for promotions to meet customer expectations efficiently. In the first instance, the promoted line needs to be available there should not be out of stock.

Effective category management takes a holistic view in planning promotions, with the intention of meeting consumer expectations without creating unnecessary inefficiencies in the system. Supported by information systems this practice has become more accurate over time.

Category Management is often exercised within a supply chain partnership context. Such partnerships between retailers and key suppliers have emerged in recent years in recognition of the substantial common interests shared by each. After all, they are both serving the same consumer.

Partnerships have longer-term perspectives where the trust between retailer and supplier has increased. In such a context, key suppliers are keen to be involved in category management, as it has strengthened their position in what can be seen as a battle over space allocation on the sales floor.

Category management is now about creating closer relationships between suppliers and retailers. But due to the complex processes the challenges facing category management are

(i) **Product Development and Sourcing:** Regional consumer preferences must be identified and products developed or sourced to satisfy these unique needs.

(ii) **Supplier Management:** This historically difficult relationship becomes even more complex, as language, cultural and commercial impediments are introduced.

(iii) **Buying:** Negotiating prices based on the true profit contribution is made more difficult by currency fluctuations, extended transportation channels and commercial practices unique to each culture.

(iv) **Merchandising:** Retailers must create the right mix of product to appeal to local needs and still have repid response processes in place when the mix must be changed or replenished.

(v) **Distribution:** This must be more diverse, with typically longer channels to move product from source to consumer. It also needs to accommodate market-specific packaging and environmental needs.

(vi) **Retail Operations:** Again, there is a need to tailor product presentation and service offerings to each specific market.

SUPPLIERS

Once the optimal merchandise mix is decided, the retailer is searching for the suppliers. A retailer can depend on one supplier (centralized) or a combination of suppliers (decentralized). The retailer may consider the various alternative sources of supply available before selecting a suitable source of supply. What is expected is, the retailer should select an effective source of merchandise from the existing alternatives. The various sources of suppliers availed by Indian retailers are,

- Manufacturers
- Wholesalers
- Agents

- Other large retailers
- Government

Whatever may be the source, careful selection of supplier will bring achievement of optimal merchandise mix by the retailer. So while selecting the supplier, the retailer must consider various criteria.

CRITERIA FOR THE SELECTION OF SUPPLIERS

Retailers regularly confront with the issue of locating a new supplier for the existing merchandise or identifying a new supplier for fresh merchandise introduced. A supplier's initial assessment will be made according to his ability to satisfy retailers in four main areas (Fig -2) together with the kind of indicators that would determine the likelihood of supplier meeting criteria. The existing suppliers may be retained because they have given particularly good service in the past, or because there is no identifiable competition. The main areas of supplier assessment criteria are:

1. Product Range and Quality

Retailers will assess the product range available with the supplier and the quality standard maintained while manufacturing or delivering. Retailers will consider the following parameters to judge the standing of a particular supplier: technical capability, design expertise, quality benchmarks, samples, and nil-defect delivery.

2. Price

Retailers will always have relative assessment of the different suppliers while deciding the purchase. At the same time, retailers as per the norms prevailing in their industry look forward to credit terms, payment options, penalties, and price points. Retailers will also evaluate the offer from the perspective of a consumer in terms of value for money and consistent price policy.

3. Delivery

In order to avoid sales loss, a retailer is generally interested in the assessment of a supplier's capacity to deliver ordered goods in time and as per specification. Retailers also evaluate the performance of the suppliers or gather information on these parameters to ascertain delivery capacity, such as minimum order quantities, lead times, workforce stability and response, and ability to collaborate on consumer-led response initiative.

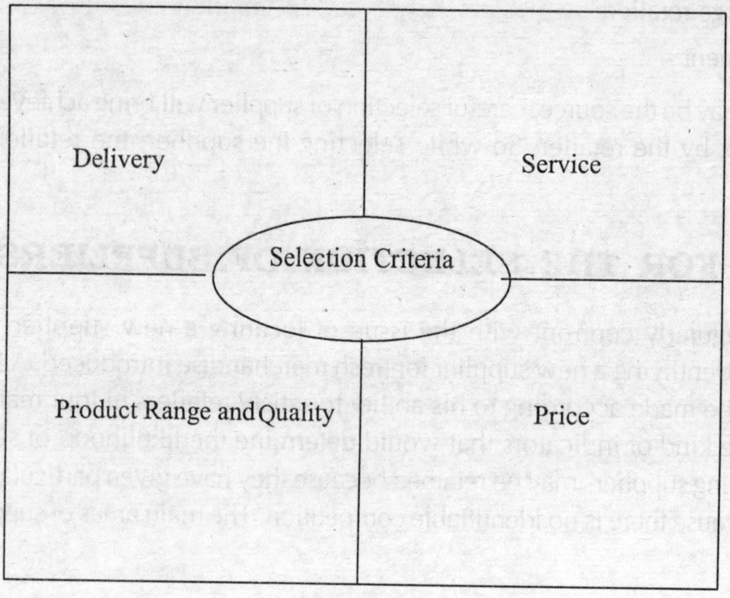

Figure 3: Selection Criteria

4. Service

This encompasses all those facilities and support extended by the supplier to add value to the goods or services, or assistance in the sale of the goods. It includes pre and post-sale services by the supplier. Retailers will be interested to assess the working of the supplier on parameters such as innovation, speed of new product or variant introduction, sampling service, marketing support (advertising and promotion), and handling queries and complaints.

A list of suppliers should be available and kept fully up to date, showing lines supplied by each. This will aid the process of review of suppliers and lines, so that suppliers performing well may be rewarded with larger orders.

BUYING SYSTEMS

Assortment Planning helps the retailer to workout a general outline on what types of merchandise should be carried. Whereas, buying systems will help the buyers and merchandise planners to decide on how much to buy. Generally retailers use two distinct types of buying systems:

(a) A staple merchandise buying systems for basics.

(b) A merchandise budget for fashion merchandise.

1. Staple Merchandise Buying Systems for Basics

Staple merchandise buying systems are used for merchandise which follow a typical (or predictable) order-receipt-order-cycle. This buying system uses past history for each staple SKU to forecast demand and sales at the category level. Most of themerchandise found in food and discount stores in addition to some categories in speciality and departmental stores like underwear, socks, *etc.*, fits this criterion.

The retailer must use the 'Inventory Management Report' containing information on sales velocity, inventory availability, amount of order, inventory turnover, sales forecast and the quantity to order for each SKU to carryout buying functions. This is because staple merchandise buying systems comprise of a number of computer programme modules to help the buyer and merchandiser to determine how much to order and when. Mainly, these systems enable buyers to carryout three functions:

- At the SKU level, monitor and measure the average current demand.
- Forecast the future SKU demand with making adjustments for seasonal fluctuations and changes in trend.
- Work out ordering decision rules for optimum restocking.

2. Merchandise Budget Plan for Fashion Merchandise

The merchandise budget plan helps to workout the inventory investment in a category over a period of time. It cannot be referred to as a complete buying plan because it does not indicate the quantities or the specific assortment to buy. The plan merely specifies how much money is to be spent each month to achieve sales and turnover and also the GMROI objectives.

The merchandise plan helps to co-ordinate the supply and demand for merchandise as well as to ensure that the financial goals are achieved. Further, the plan co-ordinates the activities of buyers of merchandise for different categories, so as to ensure that there is a balance and avoid situations where there is too much merchandise in some categories and not enough in others. Of course the actual sales may differ from the sales forecasted in the merchandise budget plan. For working out the merchandise budget plan, the buyer will have to examine the monthly sales expected as a percentage of the total sales, the factors which could reduce the inventory level (due to mark down, shrinkages, discount to employees, *etc.*), the stock-to-sales ratio at the BOM (Beginning of Month) and the GMROI. Thus, for the buyer, the GMROI, inventory turnover and the sales forecast can be used for planning and control. Based on the above inputs, the buyer will plan to purchase the merchandise for the various category levels. Fashion products can have seasonal fluctuations in demand. So, after the selling season, the buyer can understand how the category actually performed when compared to the plan for control purposes.

BUYING FUNCTION

Each and every retail store has their own unique feature. Rarely is any two stores organised in the same way. Hence, merchandising will vary from one retail organisation to another. The owner may perform the buying in a single store. As it grows, functional departmentalization may occur and number of persons involved in buying process may increase. In chain stores, the buying may be centralized or decentralized. For mail order retailing the buying may be entirely different. Buying basic merchandise is fairly different from buying fashion merchandise. Basics are always kept by the retailers, because it is always in demand., whereas fashion goods may sell very well in one season but not in demand in the next season. So the merchandiser needs to spend more time in the market looking for the products which will suit the needs of the store's consumers. It clearly indicates that the procurement of merchandise requires a basic understanding of the consumer and the retail buying environment.

Buying for a retail organisation is a critical function of merchandising. The process begins with the preparation of the buying plan, called 'Open To Buy' or OTB. It helps retailer project and control future buying so that the flow of merchandise in the store matches anticipated sales at desired stock turn rates to give a positive cash flow.

For organised buying one need to follow the OTB planning, since it prevents over-buying, eliminates confusion and enables the organisation to make more profits.

OTB refers to merchandise budgeted for purchase during a certain period of time for which the stocks have not yet been ordered. It is also the process of forecasting sales and purchases. OTB is a planning tool that assists in setting budgets for sales and merchandise inventory levels and in monitoring the current status of the OTB amount, which is the amount remaining to be ordered to meet the budget.

Every retailer needs to use OTB plan, as most tend to overstock when sales increase and understock when they are low. Often a small increase in sales leads to excessive buying that ultimately affects the retail organisation's bottom line. OTB helps a retailer fix the ideal amount of stock that should be on hand at the beginning of any given month and the quantum of new merchandise to be received during the month.

An efficient OTB plan has the following elements:

(a) Forward Sales Planning (Sales Forecast)

The sales plan ought to be prepared for the entire year with month-wise details of planned sales. A good OTB plan helps one to react to variations in sales plans (as the current month comes to an end), reschedule deliveries and cancel or alter purchase orders for future deliveries, as the case may be.

(b) Forward Cover

This is based on the planned stock turns for the retail outfit. For instance, if the planned stock turns for the store is four times in a year, and then the ideal stock holding at any point in time should be equivalent to three months' stock cover.

(c) Stock Required

This is based on the forward cover planned for the store. If the forward cover is for three months and the current month is month 1, then the stock required will be the sum of the planned/forecast sales of months 2 3 and 4.

(d) Opening Stock

The value of the opening stock is a flow calculation. In OTB planning, the first entry is an estimate. From the second month onwards, the opening stock is the closing stock figure of the previous month.

(e) Intake Requirement

This is the difference between the required stock and the opening stock.

(f) On Order

These are stocks that have been already ordered and due for delivery during the relevant period.

(g) Open to Receive

This figure is arrived at by deducting the stock on order, if any, form the intake requirement. This figure indicates the OTB quantity.

(h) Closing Stock

To arrive at this figure, one needs to take the opening stock, subtract the sales, and add the on-order and open-to-receive quantities.

Advantages of an Open to Buy Plan

1. The OTB plan enables retailers to estimate in advance the amount of working capital that needs to be employed in inventory form month to month.
2. It helps ensure the right inventory level to support planned sales and to attain the best Gross Margin Return on Inventory (GMROI)
3. The OTB plan places restraints on merchandise commitments so that the store receives the right merchandise at the right time and not before or after.
4. It enables a continuous flow of fresh merchandise into the store month after month during the season.
5. The OTB plan establishes goals so that the actual performance can be compared with the plan and corrective action taken in the required areas.

6. Above all, an efficient OTB plan provides the organisations more opportunity for profit.

Retailers who follow a well-formulated OTB plan are successful in their merchandising and buying efforts. The merchandise management system employed in the organisation generally supports such statistical techniques in the OTB plan, but it is the buyer's insight and decision making capability that help deliver the best results.

BRAND MANAGEMENT IN RETAILING

A brand can be defined as a distinguishing name or symbol such as a logo, which identifies the products or services, offered by a seller and differentiates those products and services from the offerings of competitors. In retail context, the name of the retailer will work as a brand communicating to consumers the type of merchandise and services offered by the retailers. There are some retailers who develop private label or store brands, like Wills Lifestyle, Ebony, *etc.*, which are exclusively sold through their channels. There could be single brand retailers such as Bata, Liberty Shoes, Tanishq, etc., or multibrand retailers such as Foodworld, Westside, or store brands conveying the value proposition like Big Bazaar, Fabmall, Fabmart.

In marketing parlance, a brand is a 'promise' that is made to stakeholders such as customers, investors, public, government, critics, market forces, *etc.* What finally is actually delivered once this promise has been communicated is the ultimate litmus test of the brand. Reputation is the resultant intangible asset that the corporate entity acquires at the brand contact points during the brand's engagement with its stakeholders.

According to the American Marketing Association, "A brand is a name, term, sign, symbol, or design, or a combination of them, intended to identify the goods or services of one seller and to differentiate them from those of competitors". Functionally and contextually, there are proprietary, visual, emotional, rational, and cultural images associated with a company or product

Brand management poses several challenges to the retailers. The key issues in retail branding are:

- Brand management of the retail outlet; and
- Deciding whether or not to opt for the strategy of self own branding.
- A strong retail brand and a strong private label strategy can be an effective tool to differentiate the stores and the shopping experience. Strong retail brands have a sharper definition of their brand identity in terms of the following criteria:
- Who am I?
- What do I do?
- How am I different from others?
- Why buy me?

The sharper this focus, the stronger is the retail brand. A retailer's brand is valuable since it enhances reach and endurance with the consumers, and ensures a more focused strategic plan.

Retail brands provide value to both consumers and retailers also. These could be in the form of:

- Conveying information to the prospective customers about the nature of the shopping experience, i.e., the retailer's mix which they will be treated too, while patronizing a particular retailer.
- Re-emphasize and build up the customers' confidence in their buying decisions to purchase merchandise from the retailer.
- Brands can also help to enhance customer satisfaction with the merchandise purchased by them.

Customers, usually opt for branded merchandise because of the assurance of the reliability of the company or organization name which is associated with the product or service. In fact, the value which goes with the brand image is also known as brand equity. Any merchandise with strong brand equity will be beneficial to the customer as well as the retailer.

Concept of a Brand

A brand is a promise. It say's you know the name, you can trust the promise. It is trusted only as far as those promises are met. Trust is a critical first step and brands aimed to accelerate that step leveraging the implied promise of the brand. Most of the brands have a logo which acts as a short-cut to remind us of the brand promise. The logo uses color, shape, letters and images that are designed both to catch our eyes and to guide our thoughts in the right direction. The brand may also be associated with tunes, celebrities, catchphrases and so on. All parts of the brand image works as a psychological trigger or stimulus that causes an association to all other thoughts. Powerful brands can drive success in competitive and financial markets, and indeed become the organisation's most valuable assets.

Branding Process

Branding is one of the most important issues for any business if it wants to succeed in the field of fierce competition. Branding is a collaborative process, which consists of the following five stages:

Attributes and Benefits

A brand brings to mind certain attributes, such as expensive, well-built, well-engineered, durables, etc. Attributes must be translated into functional and emotional benefits. The attribute "durable" could translate into the functional benefits like "I won't have to buy another car for several years". The attribute 'expensive' translates into the emotional benefits, "The car makes me feel important and admired."

Values

The brand also says something about the producer's value. The values related to high performance, safety, and prestige.

Culture

The brand may represent a certain culture.

Personality

The brand can project a certain personality of a person, animal or any object.

User

The brand suggests the kind of consumer who buys or uses the product we would expect to.

Brand Management

Brand Management is the application of marketing techniques to a specific product, product line, or brand. It seeks to increase the product's perceived value to the customers and thereby, increases brand franchise and brand quality. Marketers see a brand that will continue with present and future purchases of the same product. This may increase sales by making a favourable comparison with a competing product. It may also enable the manufacturer to charge more for the product. The value of the brand is determined by the amount of profit it generates for the manufacturer. This results from a combination of increased sales and increased price.

A powerful tool like a brand cannot be created in a vacuum or from thin air. It requires following certain principles and should have a developed procedure along with a well-supplemented research base. All these issues make branding a real art, which uses well-defined and established principles but can be refined as well as mastered by practice.

Brand management starts with understanding what 'brand' really means. This starts with the leaders of the company who define the brand and control its management. It also reaches all the way down to the company and especially to the people who interact with customers or who create the products that customers use. Brand management performed to its full extent means starting and ending the management of the whole company through the brand. It is comprehensive effort and requires commitment, support and contribution from each person in the company.

All the brands in a marketplace constantly view to build brand equity on a strong foundation of brand reputation. There is a direct correlation between positive brand reputation and the resultant brand equity commanded by the brand in its product category. One can think of reputed brands like Coca-Cola, Pepsi, Titan, Tanishq, Raymonds, Van Heusen, Himalaya, Cadbury, Dairy Milk, Surf Excel, Dove, Lakme, *etc.*, that have successfully overcome the competition and have emerged as stronger, victorious and trustworthy bands. What we need to remember is that competition is ultimately good for consumers at large in the marketplace. Eventually, it is the customer who stands to win amidst the brand battles. The process of building perceptual images of the brands in the minds of the consumers is very crucial and beneficial for the brand.

Johnson & Johnson (Fig - 4)is trusted by mothers across the globe. Irrespective of whether a woman is brand conscious or not, when it comes to her newborn baby, almost, every urbanite mother reposes her trust in Johnson & Johnson. Starting from the first bath which touches the very sensitive skin of the newborn, to the shampoo that touches the hair, it is Johnson & Johnson all the way.

Figure 4

The Amul moppet, which is popularly known as the 'Utterly Butterly' girl, is the evergreen symbol of Innocence and simplicity. It is as if the brand proclaims the promise of a very simple truth by innocently persuading customer with its 'round eyed, chubby cheeked' little girl happily winking at you from hoardings that are strategically placed. The brand image also implies that the product is safe for children and is vividly displayed as an innocent pleasure in consuming the product.

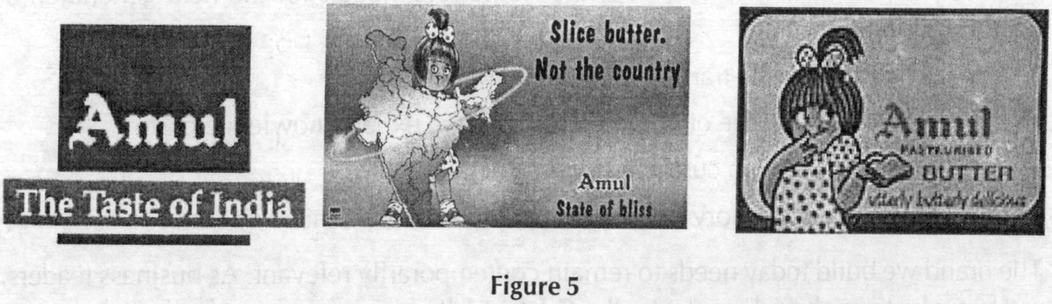

Figure 5

Maruti started its journey as a brand built for the middle-class. Today, Maruti is famous and popular across all categories of customers and is regarded as one of the best automobile companies. Maruti is popular because it is regarded as a brand that is reliable and delivers value. Brand Maruti, thus, has a very formidable reputation.

Strong brands help to over come any obstacles in the competitive market. Remember the tough times that Cadbury had to go through during its worm infestation episode. The trials and tribulations faced by a brand is almost an inflexion point of the brand, from where it refines itself – both strategically and tactically. The ultimate aim being, to progressively better the value delivered to its stakeholders. It is these tests and tribulations that forge a resilient brand . When a brand wins, all its stakeholders win. The brand, thus, acquires a reputation which results form an intricate synergy of respect, appreciation, reliability and trust that resides within its stakeholders and which ultimately ensures that the brand wins all the way till the end.

Building sustainable brand leadership is the future of marketing. Brand reputation has to be developed as a fortress that has high levels of intrinsic strength while having continuous guards on possible intrusions or threats. Continuous vigilance of brand reputation ensures sustainability and sustenance, the two strong foundations on which any brand rest.

The branding objective of any organisation should be to:

- Build brands that are sustainable across product categories so as to lessen clutter.
- Make brands achieve brand equity by linking it to brand recall, association, brand perception, and brand value.
- Build brands which have an innate esteem value.
- Build a solid brand construct that commands respect from stakeholders and the business community at large.
- Win the market share as well as the customer's heart.
- Build sustainable business and social ecosystems
- Create and encourage development of interdependent business partners creating value networks with innovative expertise.
- Consolidate on the market trust and become role-models for the next generation of business entities.
- Operate with complete transparency of operations
- Develop leadership base of human resources and expert knowledge base.
- Encourage excellence in customer-focused activities.
- Instill ethics as compulsory culture in the human and technical interface.

The brand we build today needs to remain contemporarily relevant. As business leaders, we need to evaluate our brands contextually. Contextual relevance ensures that brands convey benefits and uses that are contextually relevant to the demographics and psychographics of the target segment of the particular product. Brand reputation is the intangible asset that secures a stronghold for the marketer. Reputation, though builds on slowly, has the potential to become like diamond, capable of forging its way through incredible hard obstacles.

Change of Brand Logos for Creating New Markets

For large organisations, changing their logos is a huge exercise which has the following imperatives:

1. To be associated with the youthful.
2. To compete with global brands.
3. To upgrade within the segment brands in which the brand operates.
4. To make a shift from one product category to multiple categories.
5. For mergers or acquisitions.

For example, In Godrej Company's re-designed colorful logo, ruby (red) represents energy, emerald (green) stands for innovation and sapphire (blue) for growth. The company spent ₹ 100 crore to redefine and popularize the logo. Likewise, Ceat company also redesigned it's logo with grid in orange colour for the letter 'E'. The following figure shows clearly the change of logo adopted by the companies.

Figure 6: Change of Logos

Brand typically seeks a new identity for the following three key factors:First, and probably the most obvious factor that encourages the change is that Indian brands now have to face more competition; especially form global players and, therefore, the legacy bundle of association may not be appropriate any more. Ceat is a good example. It's new logo is more youthful in deep blue and orange, and with a simple and clutter-free design. There is an emphasis on the letter E, which represents raising the bar and signifies energy.

Second, why brands seek a new identity is associated with the need to upgrade the segment in which they operate. Godrej invested over Rs.100 crore in the rebranding exercise, including Rs.18 crores worth of advertising over six week during the Indian Premier League Cricket matches. They thought that it was the time to refresh the brand and look for a fresh positioning that appeals to the younger customers. Godrej is one of the many Indian corporate houses that is wooing the young by repositioning its brand.

Third, Brand ambitions change over time as brand move from serving one product category to becoming multi category players

BRANDING STRATEGIES

1. Manufacturer Brands

Manufacturer Brands, also known as national brands, are products designed, produced and marketed by a vendor. The manufacturer is responsible for developing the merchandise and establishing an image for the brand. In some cases, the manufacturer will use family branding strategy in which its name appears as part of the brand name for a specific product such as Godrej-Cinthal. However, some manufacturers don't associate their name with the brand.

Some retailers organised some of their categories around their most important national brands. Clothing is often organised by manufacturers brand like Levi's whereas products such as lipstick and fragrances don't insists national brands. Managing category by national brand is useful as the merchandise can be purchased in a coordinated manner around a central theme.

Buying from vendors of manufacturers brand can help store image, traffic flow and promotional expenses. Retailers buy from vendors of manufactures bands because they have the customer group who ask for the product by name. Loyal customers of manufacturer brands know what to expect from the product and feel comfortable with it. Relatively less money is required by the retailer for selling and promotional expenses for manufacturer brands.

Manufacturer brands have lower realised gross margin than private label brands, because the manufacturer promotes the brand and increase competition among retailers selling these brands. As many retailers offers the same manufacturer brands, the customers compare prices of these brands across stores. Retailers often offer significant discounts on some manufacturer brands to attract customers to their stores.

Stocking national brands may increase or decrease stores loyalty. If manufacturer brand is available in limited retail outlets customers loyalty is also limited to these stores. On the other hand, if the manufacturer brands are available from many retailers, customer loyalty may decreases because retailer cannot differentiate them from their competitors. Manufacturer brand can limit a retailer's flexibility. Vendors of strong manufacturer brands can dictate how their products art displayed, advertised, *etc.*

2. Private Brands

Private Brands also called store brands, are products developed by a retailer and available for sale only from that retailer. Retail buyers or category managers develop specifications for the merchandise and then contact with a vendor to manufacture it. The retailer is responsible for promoting the brand. Retailer's use of private brand was relatively small for several reasons as follows.

- National brands have been strongly advertised.
- It is hard for the retailer to gain economies of scale in design and production as against manufacturer brand.
- Many retailers aren't sophisticated enough to aggressively compete with manufacturer brand.
- Private brands have a reputation of being inferior to manufacturer brand.

In recent years, as the size of the retail firms has increased, private brands have assumed a new level of significance. Some retailers sell their own brands exclusively. Other retailers successfully mix manufacturer brands with their own retailer brands. A strong private brand boosts store loyalty. They can enhance store image if the private brands are of high quality and fashionable, in which case it can draw customers to their retail store. Retailers of private brands don't have that much restriction on display, promotion and pricing strategy as that of manufacturer brand.

A well run privatc label brand enhances store profitability by increasing pressure on branded manufacturers. Prices can be significantly lower and can be used to increase margins or offer products at lower prices. It ensures better control over price, delivery, and quality, and also ensures a strong brand identity for a retailer. In fact, national brands are increasingly feeling a threat from private labels. Gross margin opportunity is higher. Private brand sales have showed an increase in terms of both value and volume across countries. In most countries reviewed both household and food categories showed the highest private label penetration levels, as is expected from products whose brand loyalty is lowest. Private brands were found to be less developed in drinks and personal care products, reflecting the strength of branding in these two categories.

However, retailers need to exercise caution in cases where the national brands are too powerful and the product category is considered a high risk purchase by the consumer. Besides, private labels may not always be considered feasible where the minimum order sizes are toosmall. Although, gross margin is higher there are other expenditure like designing merchandise, creating customer awareness, developing favorable image, *etc.* Sales associates may need additional training to sell private brands against national brands. If the private brand merchandise doesn't sell the retailer cannot return it. This problem is very high for fashion merchandise. An effective private label programme should include all elements of the value proposition – price, quality, and product differentiation.

3. Bargain Branding

It targets a price sensitive segment by offering a no-frills product at a discount price. Known as generic or house brands, such unbranded, unadvertised merchandise is found mainly in drug, grocery and discount stores. It is generally perceive by the consumer to be of lower quality. Its packaging identifies it as a brand of the retailer. Bargaining branding is primarily defensive in differentiating the retailer. Its value comes from neutralizing competitors who may gain an advantage from discount pricing.

4. Premium Branding

It offers the consumer a private label at a comparable manufacturer brand quality with modest price savings. The premium brand attends to match or exceed the product quality of manufacturer brand. There is no intention to duplicate the packaging of a particular manufacturer brand. However, consumers perceive the retailer premium brand as competing manufacturer brand. To succeed the retailer must commit the resources in market research, product development, quality control and promotion to compete with manufacturer brand. Hence, development of premium branding program precludes many retailers that have few resources from diverting to this strategy.

5. Copycat Branding

It imitates the manufacturer brand in appearance and packaging, generally, is perceived to be of lower quality and offered at a lower price. By not drawing attention to the brand's origin, the copycat can confuse the consumer about the source of the product. Copycat branding is a risky private branding alternative because close copies can violate packaging and patent laws. Poor copies are ineffective.

6. Parallel Branding

It represents private labels that closely imitate the packaging and product attributes of leading manufacturer brands but with a clearly articulated "invitation to compare" in its merchandising approach and on its product label. It seeks to benefit from the brand equity of the manufacturer brand by closely imitating the national brands packaging and product qualities. However, the invitation to compare leaves little doubt that different manufacturers produce the two products. Parallel branding is a leveraging strategy used to bolster a retailer's private brand sales. The closer two products are in form, label and package, the more they are becoming substitutes. The only difference is price. This promotes the view that the parallel brands provides better value for the consumer.

To conclude, we can say whether the business is big or small brands are good. But they need to be cultivated with patience. They need proper care and convictions from the top management. Brands may help in generating incremental revenue and in creation of an identity for the business or market offering for the company. Brands are attracted in order to gain market share and this battle is dangerous yet rewarding and interesting if fought with a well chalked out strategy. Today's brand marketers are facing cut-throat competition in the domestic market particularly from retail private brands.

Questions

I. Fill in the Blanks

1. Merchandise mix is otherwise known as ________.
2. A graphical range plan is called ________.
3. For ________ buying retail need to follow OTB planning.
4. OTB stands for ________.
5. ________ is the application of marketing techniques to a specific product, product line or brand.

Answers

1. range planning 2. planogram 3. organised 4. open to buy 5. Brand Management

II. Choose the Best Answer

1. Manufacturers, wholesalers, Agent and Government are main source of ________ to Indian retailers.

   (a) buyers (b) consumers (c) suppliers (d) competitors

2. A good ________ plan helps retailer to react to various in Sales Plans.

   (a) OTB (b) OSB (c) OTP (d) TOB

3. Manufacturers brands also known as ________ brands.

   (a) private (b) stores (c) national (d) international

4. A ________ is a promise to trust the name.

   (a) logo (b) brand (c) label (d) retail store

5. _______ helps to overcome any obstacles in the competitive market.
(a) Brand (b) Store image (c) Store loyalty (d) Logo

Answers:

1. c 2. a 3. c 4. b 5. a

III. Answer in One Word

1. Expand ROI.
2. Mention the seven rights of merchandise planning.
3. What is Merchandising.?
4. What is SKU?
5. What is category?

IV. Essay Questions

1. Write an Essay on Categorizing
2. Discuss Merchandise mix in detail.
3. Who are retail suppliers? Explain the various criteria for the selection of suppliers.
4. Discuss Open To Buy (OTB) planning in detail
5. Explain the various retail branding strategies.
6. Discuss the several challenges of brand management to retailers.

Chapter 4

RETAIL PRICING

INTRODUCTION

The importance of pricing decisions is growing because today's customers are looking for good value when they buy merchandise and services. Value is the relationship of what the customer gets (goods/services) to what he or she has to pay for it. To some people, a good value means always getting a low price. Indian consumers are highly price-sensitive. Some customers are willing to pay extra as long as they believe they're getting their money's worth in terms of product quality or service.

Throughout most of history, prices were set by negotiation between buyers and sellers. Bargaining is still a sport in some areas. Traditionally, price has operated as the major determinant of buyer's choice. This is still the case in poorer nations, among poorer groups and with commodity-type products. In an economy with high levels of unemployment, with many persons living below the poverty line, the price decision takes an even greater importance. Although non-price factors have become more important in recent decades, price still remains one of the most important elements determining market share and profitability.

Price may be defined as the exchange value of goods or services in terms of money. Without price there is no marketing in the society.

What you pay is the price for what you get. Price of a product or service is what the seller feels is worth,in terms of money, to the buyer.

Price is the value that one puts on the utility that one receives for goods and services. Price in our society is generally a monetary amount, and is the value assigned to a bundle of form, time, place and possession utility. Price serves as the basis of exchange and an index of value for goods and services. The correct and incorrect price often leads to the success or failure of a product. Pricing decisions are complex and difficult. Holistic marketers must take into account many factors in making pricing decisions – the company, the customers, the competition and the marketing environment. Pricing decisions must be consistent with the firm's marketing strategy and its target markets and brand positioning. The retailer must develop a pricing strategy in a systematic manner, starting with the identification of overall pricing objectives. Objectives are necessary to achieve effective price levels. The pricing objectives must be measurable and realistic.

Setting one price for all buyers is a relatively modern idea that arouse with the development of large scale retailing. Many large scale retailers advertised 'strictly one-price policy' because they carried so many items and supervised so many employees. Retailers have responded to their customers' needs with retail formats that emphasize low prices as a means of creating a differential advantage. National discount store chains that offer everyday low prices, such as Wal-Mart, dominate many markets in many product categories. Some of the more mature retailing institutions, like department stores and supermarkets, have come to grips with these forms of price competition by adopting a more aggressive pricing strategy with a significant amount of their merchandise being sold below the manufacturers' suggested price through a strong promotion orientation. Many retailers have successfully maintained their market appeal by providing good value by offering customers high-quality merchandise and service without attempting to offer the lowest prices on a particular product category. In the middle of this price competition among national giants are the smaller retailers. Typically unable to purchase in large quantities to receive lower prices like their larger competitors, mom-and-pop retailers have either learned to use other strategies to compete or have gone out of business.

Pricing decisions are also being affected by the development of electronic channels. However, the internet also makes it easier for consumers to compare product attributes in addition to price. Due to the targeting capabilities of the electronic channel, retailers have the opportunity of charging different prices to customers on the basis of their price sensitivity. The internet has facilitated the use of an auction pricing mechanism. People have used auctions to facilitate trade for centuries. As eBay has demonstrated, no longer do auction participants have to be located at a same place.

Retailers have realized the growing importance of pricing decisions today, with customer looking for good value of their purchase. To some customers, good value means getting merchandise at a low price. While there are others who do not mind paying more as long as they feel they are getting their money's worth in terms of quality product. Retailers have responded suitably, keeping in mind the role of pricing in the growth and expansion of business. The long term pricing objectives may include the number of sales periods, the range of prices and total number to be made available and the positioning of the store and merchandise in relation to the price. Such pricing goals will convey an image of the retail outlet to the consumer based on its approach to pricing. Further, pricing has to be integrated with the other aspects of marketing mix after taking into account the target market. For example, the Pantaloon retail announced the launch of the country's biggest Food Bazaar outlet in Mumbai with an area of 20,000 Sq.ft to provide customers with new levels of standards in convenience, comfort, quantity, quality and store service. All the cooking needs of a housewife are made available under a single roof not only that the house hold items are available at wholesale price with saving in time, in a comfortable environment at value for money prices.

Pricing is an integral part of the retail strategy and cannot work in isolation. Cost and operating expenses are to be considered while establishing retail price. Price is the source of revenue to the retailers. The price of the merchandise communicates the image of the retail store to the customers. Various factors like demand for the product and target market, store policies, competition and the economic condition are to be taken into account while arriving at the price of a product. Retailers do their pricing in a variety of ways. In small retail stores, prices are often set by the boss. In large scale retailing, pricing is handled by division and product-line managers.

Some missteps in pricing are,

- Pricing is not revised often enough to capitalize on market changes.
- Price is set independently, integrated with the rest of the marketing mix.
- Price is not varied enough for different product items, market segments, distribution channels and purchase occasions.

A retailer's pricing policy must be consistent with the overall objectives and reputation of the business. The pricing policy may be in financial terms such as sales, profit, ROI or growth and expansion of business. Pricing goals are important as they provide an image of the retail outlets.

FACTORS INFLUENCING PRICING (FACTORS AFFECTING RETAIL PRICES)

1. Price sensitivity is one of the important factors which a retailer has to consider while setting retail price policy. How demand influence the price is an important consideration. To understand the demand and its influence on price, one must understand elasticity in demand process. The products which are necessities tend to be inelastic. When close substitutes are available, there is price elasticity. Large budget products tend to be elastic (e.g.) car, house purchase, whereas small budget, necessary products tend to be inelastic (e.g.) match-box, stationery item purchase. Price of the product itself can be a powerful differentiator. If consumer perceives differences, they will be highly price sensitive. Consumers show greater price sensitivity as products move through their life cycles. Price may be used as a cue to higher quality.
2. Perishable nature of product, high fashion items or products which cannot be sold in future occasion are sold by the retailers through various forms of last-minute tactical pricing or seasonal sales.
3. Competitive nature of the industry compels the retailers to set the price at competitive level or face loses of sale.
4. Cost control is important part of pricing policy. Many retailers have high fixed cost, yet they need to set competitive prices. This may lead to financial collapse if cost is not controlled.

5. Seasonal demand lead to peak price and low season requires demand management price to shift the old stock and improve cash flow position.
6. Intermediaries may influence the price through change in the cost of supply, bank charges, interest rate changes, increase in wages, *etc.*
7. Change in the government legislation may affect the retail pricing.(e.g.) VAT.
8. Volatile nature of the market due to fluctuation in international cost, problems of supply, need to stock more saleable items, catalogue price maintenance may influence retail pricing.

The pricing objectives should be in agreement with the mission statement and merchandise policies. If the purpose of the business is to maximize profit, Pricing of products must be done carefully to ensure it. The pricing objectives may be to help to achieve targeted sales, to enhance market share or to meet or prevent competition.

While arriving at the retail price, the retailer must consider the cost of goods which is the cost of merchandise and various other expenditure incurred in the movement of goods from the manufacturer to the retail store. The expenses may be fixed such as storage insurance or variable like promotional expenses. Price on the other hand, is the selling price per unit that the customer pays for the product or service. For consumers, the price of the product is the most obvious indicator of cost, hence, product price should be set carefully. The profit to be earned from the merchandise must be planned before fixing the retail price.

Retail Price = Cost + Profit

PRICING OBJECTIVES

1. Product Quality Objectives

Product quality objectives centre on recouping costs associated with retail research and development. In addition, product quality objectives can be used to create the perception of high product quality and thus high retail store quality, in the consumer's mind. This objective is often used together with a skimming objective by high-end retailers.

Example: A retailer prices items at 300 per cent above cost to ensure that its prestigious image is firmly established in the consumer's mind.

2. Skimming Objectives

With skimming objectives the retailer sets an initial relatively high price for a product. A skimming objective is often used to recoup costs incurred when selling a new product – costs associated with research, development, and marketing, for instance. The term skimming comes from dairy farms, where personnel skim the high-quality cream from the top of the milk. The cream is more valuable than the milk and can be sold at higher prices. Likewise, the product marketer skims the market with an initial high price to sell to customers who are relatively unconcerned about price. The price may be lowered later to attract additional customers who are more price conscious. With this strategy, the customer must be somewhat price insensitive and view the product or service as premium quality.

Example: A retailer initially prices a DVD player at ₹ 3750. After a period of six months, the cost will be lowered to ₹ 2500. Once competitors enter the market, the price will be set to remain competitive

3. Market Penetration Objectives

Market Penetration Objectives are the opposite of skimming objectives. Prices are initially set lower to attract large numbers of customers. Market penetration objectives are effective when the retailer's customers are price sensitive. The key to an effective market penetration strategy is to increase sales volumes to offset the low product price. As a general rule, after a certain point, retail costs do not increase very much when sales volume increases. Market penetration objectives have the added benefit of allowing the retailer to discourage competition from entering the trading area because of the lower prices the retailer has already established for the market. In addition, market penetration may help establish a new product as a popular alternative for the consumer, thus, creating social pressure to own the product as well as an economic benefit.

Example: A retailer sets prices at lower levels for the first two months of operation to increase market share and discourage competition.

4. Market Share Objectives

Market Share Objectives allow the retailer to adjust price levels based on competitors' changes in price, enabling the retailer to create additional market share or reduce market share in relation to the competition. This can be done for the entire retail operation (that is, all stores), for a division, or for a specific store. The retailer can also set a market share objective for each department, product line or product and brand.

Example: To stand by its "we will not be undersold" policy, a retailer sets its average prices below those of its three main competitors.

5. Survival Objectives

Survival Objectives allow the retailer to increase price levels to meet sales expenses. This type of objective is generally used to match sales volumes to overall store (or company) expenses.

Example: A retailer sets pricing to cover expenses and increase store profitability over last year's by 5 per cent.

6. Return on Investment (ROI) Objectives

Return on Investment (ROI) Objectives is created to help the retailer meet or exceed stated return on investment figures. Management creates a target return figure it thinks will be satisfactory to stakeholders. Then the price is set to reach that targeted return level.

ESTABLISHING RETAIL PRICE

Retailers want to set prices to maximize long-term profits. To do this, they need to consider the following: (1) cost, because they want to make a profit, (2) demand, because this is what customers will pay for the merchandise, and (3) competition, because customers shop around and compare prices. Thus, pricing strategy adopted by a retailer can be cost-oriented, demand-oriented or competition oriented

Cost Oriented Pricing

Under the cost-oriented method, the retail price is determined by adding a fixed percentage to the cost of the merchandise. In Cost-oriented pricing, a basic markup is added to the cost of the merchandise to arrive at the price. Here, retail price is considered to be a function of the cost and markup.

Thus, Retail Price = Cost + Markup,

If this formula is rearranged, we get

Cost = Retail Price – Markup and,

Markup = Retail Price – Cost.

The difference between the selling price and the cost is considered as the markup and should cover for the operating expenses and transportation etc. Markup percentages may be calculated on the retail price or on the cost. They are calculated as under:

Markup % (at retail) = [Retail Selling Price – Merchandise Cost]/Retail Selling Price

Markup % (at cost) = [Retail Selling Price – Merchandise Cost]/Merchandise Cost

When the retailer is aware of the markup percentage required and the selling price, he can also work out the price at which he actually needs to procure the product.

Sometimes, it may not be possible to adopt the policy of maintaining a single markup for a product category, then the concept of a variable markup policy can be followed. This allows the retailer to procure goods at varying prices, but at the same time, maintain the margins that need to be earned, as some products may earn a higher margin while others, a lower margin.

Demand Oriented Pricing

With the demand-oriented method, prices are based on what customers expect or are willing to pay. Demand oriented pricing focuses on the quantities that the customers would buy at various prices. It largely depends on the perceived value attached to the product by the customer. Sometimes, a high priced product is perceived as a high quality product and a low priced product is perceived as of low quality. An understanding of the target market and the value proposition that they would look for is the key to demand oriented pricing.

Competition Oriented Pricing

With the competition-oriented method, prices are based on competitors' prices. When the prices adopted by the competitors play a key role in determining the price of the product, it is said that Competition Oriented Pricing is being followed. Here, the retailer may price the product on par with the competition, above the competitor's price or below it.

Which method is best? The answer is all three! The cost-oriented method's strength is that it is quick, mechanical, and relatively simple to use. Retailers use it because they are making thousands of pricing decisions each week and cannot take the time to thoroughly analyze and determine the best price for each product.

The demand-oriented method's strength is that it allows retailers to determine which price will give them the greatest profit. But demand-oriented pricing is hard to implement, especially in a retailing environment with thousands of SKUs that require individual pricing decisions.

The competition-oriented method should be considered because it is always important to keep in mind what the competitor is doing . The degree to which a retailer sets the market price or follows the market leader is, however, a complicated issue.

Retailers need to consider costs, demand, and competition in setting prices. The cost-oriented method would be the starting point for setting a price. The competition-oriented method provides an outside check on the marketplace. The demand-oriented method is then used for fine-tuning the strategy. Retailers would start with a price based on costs and their profit goals, consider competition, and then perform tests to determine if it's the most profitable price.

RETAIL PRICING POLICIES

The pricing polices that may be adopted by a retailer include:

Cost Plus Pricing

For the Cost Plus method price will be in relation to either marginal cost or total cost including the overheads. The approach includes:

- Select the target market
- Determine the cost of the goods in store-storage cost, selling cost, shrinking estimates, overheads, etc.
- Determine the ceiling price above which the retailer would be offering expensive prices compared with those of competitors.

- Apply the markup, given that the possible range has been identified in order to achieve profit objectives. There may be some discretion for pricing individual items within a department as it is the overall profit which is important. A percentage markup is normally applied to reach the final selling price. This may be expressed as a percentage of cost or selling price.

Rate of Return Pricing

This is another cost oriented pricing method. This method concentrate on the profits generated in relation to the capital invested. This approach ignores the need to link the pricing policy to the creation of a sales volume which is larger enough to cover overheads or to ensure that demand will remain consistent over time. Cost plus or rate of return pricing method is not appropriate for those retail products which have to survive in a highly competitive market place

Backward Pricing

This is a market based method of pricing which focuses on what the consumer is willing to pay. First an acceptable margin is agreed upon. Next the costs are closely monitored so that the price which is deemed to be acceptable is able to be matched. If necessary an adjustment is made to the quality of the product to meet the cost lead needs of this technique. Retailers selling on a price lead basis often insist that their suppliers meet specific costs even if this compromises some aspects of quality. This approach can be associated with price lining. Price lining is the method of simplifying the merchandise comparison for the customer by establishing a number of lines within price points for each classification. Once the price line have been determined the retailers purchase goods which fits into each line. In order to be successful, the price lines have to be large enough to reflect a value difference for the consumer. It helps to convince the customer either for trading up or for trading down. The benefit of limiting the number of price lines is that a retailer can achieve broader assortments which leads to increased sales and fewer markdowns. Price lining help the retailer to increase the sales volume by having larger assortments, there is clarity of price, line concentration pave the way for improved display and control is becoming easier.

Market Skimming

The strategy here is to charge initial high prices and then reduce them gradually, if at all. A skimming price policy is a form of price discrimination over time and for it to be effective, several conditions must be met. The success of a price-skimming strategy is largely dependent on the inelasticity of the demand for the product either by the market as a whole, or by certain market segments. The main objective of employing a price-skimming strategy is to benefit from high short-term profits (due to the newness of the product) and from effective market segmentation. Such a strategy for pricing of products works well when the products are considered to be prestige goods or luxury items.

Market Penetration

This strategy is the opposite of market skimming and aims to capture a large market share by charging low prices. The low prices charged stimulate purchases and can discourage competitors from entering the market as the profit margins per item are low. Retailers who wish to enter a new market or build on a relatively small market share, often use this strategy. This will only be possible where the demand for the product is believed to be highly elastic, i.e., demand is price-sensitive and either new buyers will be attracted or existing buyers will buy more of the product as a result of the low price.

Expansionistic Pricing

It is another form of penetration pricing. Under this strategy, the product enjoys a high price elasticity of demand so that the adoption of a low price leads to significant increases in sales volumes. Companies attempting to enter new or international markets for their products, may use expansionistic pricing strategies. A low cost version of a product may be offered at a very low price, to gain recognition and acceptance by consumers. Once acceptance has been achieved, more expensive versions or models of the offering can be made available at higher prices.

Competitive Pricing

It is employed to match the market prices of competitive retailers. This is a technique which requires knowledge of actual cost as matching the pricing of a more efficient retailer may lead to loses on particular item. It also requires an understanding of the importance of the pricing policies of the competitor from a consumer perspective. A retailer with a strong brand image does not necessarily need to match competitor's offers.

Leader Pricing

In leader pricing, the retailer sells one or a few items at a deep discount to increase traffic and sales on complementary items. The key to successful leader pricing is that the product must appeal to a large number of people and should appear as a bargain. The best items for this type of pricing are those frequently purchased by shoppers, e.g., bread, eggs, milk, etc. Some retail items may be priced very competitively so as to sacrifice profit on specific items in order to generate more overall demand for other items. These are often known as loss leaders if they are sold below cost but in reality retailers seldom make a cash loss on the items even though they are heavily discounted. The leader items are sold near to cost rather than at loss. The purpose behind the use of leader price is to increase store visits, purchases and the perception of good value. If the customers are limiting their purchase to the lead items, the price promotion need to be revised.

Every Day Low Pricing

Every Day Low Pricing or EDLP as it is popularly known, is a strategy adopted by retailers who continually price their products lower than other retailers in the area. Many retailers have adopted an everyday low pricing (EDLP) strategy. This strategy emphasizes continuity of retail prices at a level somewhere between the regular non sale price and the deep-discount sale price of the retailer's competitors. The term everyday low pricing is therefore somewhat of a misnomer. Low doesn't necessarily mean lowest. Although retailers using EDLP strive for low prices, they aren't always the lowest price in the market. At any given time, a sale price at a competing store or a special purchase at a wholesale club store may be the lowest price. A more accurate description of this strategy is therefore every day same prices because the prices don't have significant fluctuations.

The famous example of EDLP is Wal-Mart, who regularly follow this strategy. The objective is to assure buyers that they need not wait for a sale or promotion to achieve attractive prices across the range of products they want to buy. With this strategy, retailers assume that consumers are attracted by their focus on low priced products, rather than by marketing initiatives. EDLP is a strategy which is open to large operators who have significant economies of scale and buying power. Since it is difficult to always have the lowest prices, some retailers have adopted a **low price guarantee policy** in which they guarantee that they will have the lowest possible price for a product or a group of products. The guarantee usually promises to match or better any lower price found in the local market. The promise normally includes a provision to refund the difference between the seller's offer price and the lowest price.

This method offer number of benefits

- EDLP allows retailers to withdraw from sales period price wars and create a market position that imparts fairness of pricing. Once customers realize that prices are fair, they'll buy more each time and buy more frequently.
- The stable EDLP eliminates the need for communicating special price offers and thus reduce the retailer's advertising expenditure. Also, catalogs don't become obsolete as quickly since prices don't changes as often
- Sales staff are able to spend adequate time in dealing with customers as the demand for their retail products is less seasonal and volatile. It ensures better customer service.
- EDLP reduces more variation in demand. With more even demand it is easy to control the stock situation. In addition, a more predictable customer demand pattern enables the retailer to improve inventory turnover by reducing the average inventory turnover by reducing the average inventory needed for special promotions and backup stock.
- If the retailer impart an image of fair pricing, the overall effect can be increase in stock turnover and profitability.

EDLP has some major benefits to recommend it; however, it would not be appropriate for all retailers. Some retailers would find it difficult to maintain low prices for a continuous period because of a lack of economies of scale in buying or the competitive nature of their business. Also, retailers selling goods which have a strong fashion content are more likely to want to set initial prices at a high level as this is good business practice.

High/Low Pricing

In a high/low pricing strategy, retailers offer prices that are sometimes above their competition's EDLP, but they use advertising to promote frequent sales. The sales undertaken by retailers using high/low strategies have become more intense in recent years. In the past, fashion retailers would mark down merchandise at the end of a season;grocery and drugstores would have sales only when their vendors offered them special prices or when they were overstocked. Today, many retailers respond to increased competition and a more value-conscious customer by promoting more frequent sales.

A high/low strategy has several strengths to it like:

- **The same Merchandise Appeals to Multiple Markets**

High/low strategy allows retailers to charge higher prices to customers who are not price-sensitive and lower prices to price-sensitive customers. When fashion merchandise first hits the store, it's offered at its highest price. Fashion leaders, those who are less sensitive to price, and hard-to-fit customers often buy as soon as the merchandise is available. As the season progresses and markdowns are taken, more price-sensitive customers enter the market and pay a lower price for the same merchandise. Finally, hard-core bargain hunters enter the market for the end-of-season deep-discount sales. Some customers pay little attention to the prices they pay; others will wait for merchandise to go on sale and stockpile for future use.

- **Sales Create Excitement**

A "get them while they last" atmosphere often occurs during a sale. sales draw crowds, and crowds create excitement. Some retailers augment low prices and advertising with special in-store activities like product demonstrations, giveaways, and celebrity appearances.

- **Sales move Merchandis**

All merchandise will eventually sell – the question is, at what price? Frequent sales enable retailers to move the merchandise, even though profits erode.

- **Emphasis is on Quality**

A high initial price sends a signal to customers that the merchandise is high quality. When merchandise goes on sale, customers still use the original, or reference price to gauge quality. An EDLP policy may send the wrong signal to customers. They may assume that since prices are low, quality or services may suffer. But high/low pricing helps to compare with original price, during sale.

Odd Pricing

This is otherwise known as psychological pricing. Retailers will often price products below a round figure. Retail prices are set in such a manner that the prices end in odd numbers, such as ₹ 99.99 or ₹ 199, ₹ 299, etc. Odd pricing is used to denote lower sale prices. However, there is no conclusive evidence that such pricing policies make any significant difference to profits.

Single Pricing

In this situation, the retailer charges the same price for the same product under similar circumstances. This policy is also sometimes referred to as one-price policy. A common example of this strategy is the dollar shops in USA, which charge one price for a variety of items sold. In TamilNadu, the hand cart sellers, sell variety of plastic household articles charging one price for the variety of items handled by them.

PRICE ADJUSTMENTS

Retailers are relatively free to promote adjustments to the initial retail price with the hope of generating sales. Markdowns, Coupons, Rebate, Price Bundling, Multiple-unit pricing, Variable pricing and Internet pricing are the ways through which price adjustments are carried out by the retailers.

Markdowns

Markdowns are reductions in the retail price. It is a type of second degree price discrimination because the lower price induces price sensitive customers to buy more merchandise. There are many reasons to adopt markdowns by retailers which is classified as either clearance or promotional. Many retailers think of markdowns as mistakes. When merchandise is a slow moving, absolute, at the end of selling season or priced higher than competitors goods, it generally gets markdown for clearance purposes. Sometimes this merchandise can become an eyesore and impair a store's image. Retailers employ markdowns to promote merchandise, to increase sales. A retailer may decide to markdown some merchandise to make room for something new. An additional benefit is that the markdown sale generates cash flow to pay for new merchandise. Markdowns are also taken to increase customers' traffic flow. Retailers plan promotions in which they take markdowns for holidays, for special events and as part of their overall promotional programme. Markdowns also increase the sale of complementary products. Retailers have traditionally created a set of arbitrary rules for taking markdowns. For example, one retailer adopt markdown when their weekly sales percentage fall below a certain value. Another retailer cut prices on the basis of how long the merchandise has been in the store – marking products down by 20% after 8 weeks, 30% after 12 weeks, *etc.* But such rule base approach is limited in several ways. Instead of relying on rules, a retailer can benefit significantly from optimization software. Merchandising optimization software is a set of algorithms that monitors merchandise sales, promotions, competitor's action and other factors to determine the optimum price and timing for merchandising markdowns. The optimization software works by constantly refining its pricing forecasts on the basis of actual sales throughout the season. Retailers must work closely with their vendor partners to co-ordinate deliveries and help share the financial burden of taking markdowns. Retailers can reduce the amount of markdowns by closely working with the vendors to time deliveries with demand. Merchandise that arrives ahead of times when it is needed takes up valuable selling space and can be damaged. When merchandise arrives too late, retailers may have trouble selling it without extensive markdowns. Quick response inventory system reduce the lead time for receiving merchandise so that retailers can closely monitor changes in trends and customer demand, thus, reducing markdowns. Vendors have a vested interest in retailers' success. Vendors having good knowledge about the market competition can help the retailer in stock selections. Retailer at the same time must trust their own taste and intuition so that their merchandise differs from other retail stores. Marked down merchandise can be consolidated in number of ways. The consolidation can be made into one or few of the retailers' regular locations. The marked down merchandise can be consolidated into another retail chain or an outlet under the same ownership.

Coupons

Coupons offer a discount on the price of specific items when they are purchased at a store. Coupons are also considered to be second degree price discrimination because they provide an incentive to price sensitive customers to purchase more merchandise. Coupons are issued by retailers through newspapers, on products, on the shelf, at the cash register, over internet or through mail. Coupons induce customers to try products for the first time, convert the first time users into regular user, encourage large purchase, increase usage and protect the retailer's market share. Since, coupons have a positive effect encouraging large purchases it may be stealing sales from a future period without any net increase in sales. For example in a supermarket, a coupon promotion on sugar encourages large purchase and stockpiles it for future use. Thus, the net impact on sales will be negligible and it will have negative impact on profit by the amount of the redeemed coupons. Some believe that coupons annoy, alienate and confuse consumers and therefore, do little to increase store loyalty

Rebates

A rebate is a portion of the purchase price returned to the buyer. Generally, the customer sends a proof of purchase to the manufacturer or a rebate clearinghouse that processes rebates for the manufacturer, and the customer is sent the rebate. Rebates are most useful when the amount is relatively large. Otherwise, it's not worth the customer's time and postage to redeem the rebate. For instance, rebates are often offered on cars, computers, and electronic products.

From the retailer's perspective, rebates are more advantageous than coupons since they increase demand in the same way coupons may, but the retailer has no handling costs.

Manufacturers like rebates because many consumers never bother to redeem them. Many advertisements prominently proclaim low prices, noting the requirement to send in for rebates in microscopic letters. Consumers are drawn to the store and purchase the product, but only 5 to 10 per cent claim the rebate.

Manufacturers also like rebates because they let them offer price cuts to consumers directly. With a traditional price cut, retailers can keep the price on the shelf the same and pocket the difference. Rebates can also be rolled out and shut off quickly. Buyers are required to fill out forms with names, addresses, and other data. Rebates become a great way to build a customer data warehouse.

Price Bundling

This form of pricing is a variation of multiple pricing, where various products are bundled together and sold as one unit. The products are put together as a package deal and are charged a single price. Price Bundling is the practice of offering two or more products for sale at one price. For e.g., In India, Johnson & Johnson company offering Johnson baby pack which consists of various products for the new born baby. The price bundle range from ₹ 51 to ₹ 501 depending upon the number of items in the bundle. The price bundle strategy can also be used to move less desirable merchandise by including it in a package with merchandise in high demand. For e.g., In Tamilnadu, through fair price shops, 10 grocery items put in one bundle of pack priced at ₹ 50. Other examples of this type of pricing include fast food restaurants putting together and offering of products under Happy Price menu or a computer hardware manufacturer selling the hardware and printer and some software at a particular price as a package.

Multiple-unit Pricing

Multiple-unit pricing is similar to price bundling in that the lower total merchandise price increases sales, but the products or services are similar rather than different. For example, one T-shirt may be priced for ₹ 255.99 while two t-shirts may be offered at ₹ 355.99 or a can of soft drink may be priced at ₹ 15, while a pack of three may be sold for ₹ 40. Like price bundle, this strategy is used to increase sales volume. Depending on the type of product, customers may stockpile for use at a later time. If customers stockpile, demand is shifted back in time with no long-term effect on sales. In multi unit pricing, the retailer offers discounts to customers who buy in large quantity or who buy a product bundle. This involves value pricing for more than one of the same item. Multi unit pricing usually helps move products which are slow moving. Under this pricing strategy, the customer is given a discount for making quantity or bulk purchase. This is an example of psychological pricing where the customer believes that he is getting a bargain for buying more units.

Variable Pricing

It is otherwise known as discrimination pricing or zone pricing or flexible pricing. It is often used when products are sold at two or more different prices. Variable pricing means charging different prices in different stores, markets or zones . Quite often students, the unwaged and older people are charged lower prices than other consumer segments. A garage will offer different prices for servicing company cars as opposed to private cars. A customer known to a retailer may be given a personal discount as a part of a flexible approach to pricing based upon a personal relationship with that individual. Discrimination pricing is often time related, for example, cheaper meal prices in early evening hours prior to high demand periods.

Retailers generally use variable pricing to face different competitive situation in their various markets. While this may be necessary in the short run to face the highly competitive market, it may cause ill will among customers who purchase from different multiple channels. For e.g., Food retailers often have four or five price zones in a single city. Prices can vary as much as 10% depending upon the competition and economic health of the neighbourhood. Variable pricing is easier in food and drug retail sector than for other stores because many do not item price-put a price tag on each item. It is easy to have different prices in various stores because it is so easy to change them. Variable pricing also doesn't conflict with their promotional strategy because many newspapers print different editions where advertisement are printed at a retailer's expense and distributed as an insert in the newspaper. There are some problems associated with variable pricing like customers who shop at different stores may get confused regarding prices and from a managerial point of view, it is difficult to keep track of different prices for the same item in different stores. For price discrimination to be successful, it is necessary to be able to identify those segments which, without the price differentials, would not purchase the product. Discrimination may also be based upon increasing the price of the product which has higher potential demands. For example, on Valentines' or Mothers' day the price of flower is raised.

Internet Pricing

In the mid-1990s, when e-retailing was in its infancy, internet retailers used low prices to attract customers and make them loyal. Other retailers offered coupons. Many start-up e-retail firms invested huge sum of money in this low-margin pricing strategy, never making a profit and ultimately going out of business.

Although internet pricing is not all about low pricing, some strategies pursued by the e-retailers are different than those found in traditional retailing. Auctions sales through eBay gained momentum. Auctions are particularly good for merchandise whose value is unclear, such as antiques, damaged or returned goods and fashion goods which are old and out of season products. Auctions enable sellers to locate and sell to the highest bidder. The auction site eBay has revolutionized the way many web surfers spend their time and money. Many retailers used eBay to auction their overstocked, returned, and out-of–season merchandise. eBay has created a worldwide market for small retailers of specialized or collectable merchandise. Internet is a great tool for comparisons shoppers who can click around looking for great prices. Even though customers say they shop around for low prices, many customers visit only one or two sites. Internet retailing is no longer all about low prices.

MERCHANDISE ALLOCATION

Once the merchandise is purchased and priced, it must be allocated to stores. Most retailers classify their stores as A, B or C, based on their sales potential. Each chain's allocation of merchandise to stores is different, but it should be based on the total number of stores in the chain and the distribution of sales among the stores. Each store, regardless of size, must carry a large proportion of the assortment offered; otherwise, the customers will perceive the smaller stores as having an inferior assortment.

The stores which are larger and amount for a larger percentage of the sales, can get merchandise more frequently. The seasonality of demand in each store, the amount of time that it takes for the merchandise to reach the locations, specific colors and sizes, all must be taken into account while allocating the merchandise.

The retail buying process has traditionally been reviewed from a rational or scientific method of vendor selection. However, the subjective nature of consumers requires that merchandising decisions incorporate the skill and intuition of second-guessing customers' future wants, needs and desires. Retail consumers can be very subjective in their buying decisions.

Inventory is one of the major assets of a retail firm and plays a vital role in the operations and profitability of the firm. As the number of suppliers and stock keeping units (SKUs) increase, the significance of inventory increases. While larger organisations typically give a formal role to merchandising, (*i.e.*, specialized departments and buying centres), the importance of buying decisions is frequently discounted. Catering to the changing needs and desires of the consuming public requires the skill and intuition of second-guessing customers. Often, small businesses are resource poor; therefore, even monitor miscalculations in planning, control, or merchandising decisions can be catastrophic.

EVALUATING MERCHANDISE PERFORMONCE

Measuring the performance of merchandise is necessary in order to gain an understanding of the products which have performed well and which have not performed as per the target. The performance can be as per plan, below the plan or above the plan.

Inventory turnover, which may also be called inventory or merchandise stock turn or just turnover, is a key to merchandise performance. Inventory turnover measures how long inventory is on-hand before it is sold. Items that are on-hand for a short time have a high turnover, those that are on-hand longer have a low turnover.

Retailers calculate inventory turnover in several ways:

1. Net sales/average inventory at retail
2. Cost of merchandise sold/average inventory at cost.
3. Units sold/average units in inventory
4. Net sales = turnover x average inventory at retail
5. Average inventory at retail = net sales/turnover

Turnover is a key to high performance, which means profits in retailing. However, higher turnover does not indefinitely increase profits, and the lowest turnover will not necessarily result in the lowest profits.

Rapid turnover enables the retailer to reduce certain expenses. Lower inventories will obviously require less capital, and thus, the retailer's interest expense will be lower. Also associated with lower inventories will be lower levels of required insurance coverage, lower inventory taxes on year-end inventories and lower cost of space to store the inventory. On the other hand, rapid turnover can increase expense. With similar average inventories on hand, the retailer must order more frequently and in smaller quantities, resulting in higher clerical costs, lost quantity discounts and higher transportation rates.

Success in retail can be measured by the amount of profit generated in relation to the working capital invested – the return on investment. Certain costs in any business are fixed. Shop rents and head office costs fall into this category. Merchandise margins and the product mix, however, are variable, and their management can either enhance or destroy profitability.

There are three methods of analyzing merchandising performance:

1. ABC analysis
2. Sell Through analysis
3. Multiple Attribute method

ABC Analysis

ABC analysis rank orders merchandise by some performance measure to determine which items should never be out of stock, which items should occasionally be allowed to be out of stock and which items should be deleted from the stock selection. An ABC analysis can be done at any level of merchandise classification, from an SKU to a department.

ABC analysis utilizes the 80:20 principle, which implies that 80% of the sales come from 20% of the products. The first step in the ABC analysis is to rank order SKUs using one or more criteria. The most important performance measure for this type of analysis is Contribution margin.

Contribution is calculated as follows:

Net sales	xxxx
Less: Cost of goods sold	xxx
Gross Profit	xxx
Less: Variable expenses	xx
Contribution	xxx

The next step is to determine how items with different levels of profit or volume should be treated differently. The buyer may define as A items that account for 5% of items and represent 70% of sales. B items represent 20% of items and 20% of sales. C items account for 75% of the SKU's, but contribute only 10% of sales.

Sell through Analysis

A sell through analysis is a comparison between the actual and planned sales, to determine whether early markdowns are required or whether more merchandise is needed to satisfy the demand. There is no rule which can determine when a markdown is necessary. It depends on experience with the merchandise in the past, or whether the merchandise is scheduled to be featured in some advertising, or whether the vendor can reduce the buyer's risk by providing markdown money, etc.

If actual sales stay significantly ahead of planned sales, a reorder should be made.

Multiple Attribute Method

This method uses a weighted average score for each vendor. The following steps are followed:

(a) Develop a list of issues to consider for decision-making – e.g., vendor reputation, service, merchandise quality, selling history, etc.

(b) Give importance weights to each attribute

(c) Make judgments about each individual brand's performance on each issue.

(d) Combine the importance and performance scores.

(e) Add all to arrive at the brand scores.

CONCEPT OF GROSS MARGIN RETURN ON INVESTMENT (GMROI)

Many retailers use the performance indicators of gross margin % (after mark down) and week's cover to measure performance. While the gross margin % is a measure of the relative profitability without taking into account, the costs of stockholding investment, Week's cover tells us how effectively, the stock was turned, without informing us about the relative profitability. What is needed is a measure that combines these two indicators into an indicator of real profitability GMROI gives us this.

GMROI is Calculated as Gross Margin/Average Inventory at Cost

GMROI is a merchandise planning and decision making tool that assists the buyer in identifying and evaluating whether an adequate gross margin is being earned by the products purchased, as compared to the investment in the inventory required to generate the gross margin. It focuses the buyers' attention on return-on-investment rather than on sales as a basis for merchandising decisions. The focus is on SKU's (stock keeping units) of each individual product rather than department totals and it helps identify product "winners" and core products.

Product winners are those products which perform well, which boost profitability and are the best-return-on-investment products. Core products on the other hand, are the buyer's list of existing winners that can never be out of stock. They're the most valuable products in terms of their high profitability and their excellent return on investment.

Gross margin is the value of sales less the cost of goods sold. Increasing gross margin entails increasing the sales revenue or reducing the cost of the merchandise. The obvious way to increase sales revenue is simply to increase prices. Unfortunately, in a competitive environment, things are not that easy. The recommended approach is to avoid products that are known value items or those that your competitors focus on for price comparisons. Merchandise managers who can effectively inter-relate gross merchandise management and inventory turnover management will be able to achieve high performance results.

Another method of managing inventory investments is to predetermine the stock levels at which merchandise should be recorded. This is known as the reorder point. Various factors like the lead time required, the safety stock and the speed at which the products sell, have to be taken into consideration. It may not always be possible for a retail buyer to place orders for products in small quantities; hence the Economic Order Quantity (EOQ) is determined. For this purpose, it is necessary to first determine the sales for the products, then take into consideration various factors like cost, discounts and cost of holding inventory and the Economic Order Quantity is (EOQ) determined. The EOQ is calculated by using the following formula

$$EOQ = \sqrt{2AO/C}$$

Where, A = Annual consumption

O = Ordering cost

C = Carrying cost per unit per annum

The EOQ model assumes that the unit cost of an item is constant, irrespective of the quantity of the order placed. In practice, for large order, quantity discounts in price and transportation costs are given. Such discounts cannot be accounted for in the EOQ model.

Many a times, the retailer may also use the concept of **Direct Product Profit (DPP)** to measure the performance of a product. DPP focuses on the contribution profit of individual retail items in individual stores. DPP equals an item's gross margin, plus discounts and allowances earned, less direct handling, selling and inventory holding costs. DPP enables the retailer to develop results for brands, categories, departments, stores, etc., thus forming the basis for merchandising decisions.

By expressing DPP in a common unit of measure (floor space), retailers can compare the performance of products of different physical proportions. Since retail space is usually limited, DPP can be used for:

1. Item selection (high DPP items should generally be added, low ones reviewed with an eye toward pruning)
2. Store/shelf location (high DPP items should be given prime location), and
3. Promotion (total DPP can be improved by increasing the sales of high DPP products).

CONSUMER RESPONSES TO PRICES

While setting retail prices, it is important to understand the impact of various place points on demand. In this context, the various price elasticity's need to be factored in for the calculation of price. While price elasticity is a characteristic of the product, price sensitivity is a characteristic of the consumer. Price sensitivity in turn affects price elasticity.

Price Elasticity

Price elasticity of an offering plays a key role in price fixing. Price elasticity determines the extent to which the demand for an offering responds to a change in price. Retailers are required to find out whether customers would continue to buy their offerings even when the price is high, *i.e.*, whether a significantly more numbers of customers will buy the product if the price is low.

If an offering is price elastic, a change in price will cause an even larger change in the quantity demanded. This usually means that if a retailer lowers price of its merchandise, the quantity demanded of a product or service will increase. However, some products may see an increase in demand as prices are raised due to a perception of higher quality and luxury.

The retailers should take due care in setting the price of price elastic products. If the item is more expensive than the competitors', be sure there are added features and benefits to make up for the different. If the retailer is selling a price-inelastic product or service, a change in price will cause less of a change in quantity demanded. So, whatever price you charge, your demand will be relatively stable. Items that are price inelastic usually have no similar items available, and no substitutions for the products exist. Because of this, proprietors with price inelastic products have the ability to charge a higher price.

Price Sensitivity

To determine retail prices, the price sensitivity of the customers needs to be determined. Price sensitivity is influenced by a number of factors such as substitute awareness effect and income effect.

When there are a lot of substitutes available to the customers, and comparing prices among them is easy, the price sensitivity is high. The customers can switch easily if they perceive that the price they are paying is high.

The customers are price sensitive when the expenditure incurred on a particular product is high. The expenditure is large both in terms of absolute rupees as well as percentage of the customers' income.

Pricing is a critical decision for the retailer. Pricing strategy must be determined after considering the business objectives and the various external factors that impact the validity of the decision. The increasing role of technology in retail business is also offering a set of varied alternatives to the retailer to fine-tune prices in accordance with market segment and merchandise features.

Questions

I. Fill in the Blanks

1. What you pay is the __________ for what you get.
2. __________ is the exchange value of goods or services in terms of money.
3. __________ is an integral part of the retail strategy and cannot work in isolation.
4. __________ objective allow the retailer to increase price to meet sales expenses.
5. __________ oriented pricing focuses on the quantities that the customer would buy at various prices.

Answers

1. price 2. Price 3. Pricing 4. Survival 5. Demand

II. Choose the Best Answer

1. Pricing objectives should be in agreement with the __________ policies.
   (a) product (b) merchandise (c) sales (d) buying
2. Market share objective allow the retailer to adjust their price base on __________ price
   (a) wholesaler (b) government (c) competitor (d) market
3. In __________ pricing, a basic markup is added to the cost of merchandise to arrive at price.
   (a) cost oriented (b) demand oriented
   (c) competitive oriented (d) market oiented
4. Charging initial high price is __________ price policy.
   (a) penetration (b) skimming (c) leader (d) everyday low
5. Price the product lower than other retailer in the area is __________ pricing.
   (a) penetration (b) skimming (c) leader (d) everyday low

Answers

1. b 2. c 3. a 4. b 5. d

III. Answer in One Word

1. Expand ROI.
2. What is cost oriented pricing?
3. What is price lining?
4. What is price range?
5. Explain EDLP

IV. Essay Questions

1. Define pricing. Discuss the various factors affecting retail prices.
2. Explain the various pricing objectives.
3. Discuss the various retail pricing policies.

Chapter

5 RETAIL LOCATION STRATEGIES

INTRODUCTION

Location is the most important ingredient for any business that relies on customers. It is also one of the most difficult to plan completely. Location decisions can be complex, costs can be quite high, there is often little flexibility once a location has been chosen, and the attributes of location have a strong impact on a retailer's overall strategy. A good location may let a retailer succeed even if its strategy mix is mediocre.

The choice of a location requires extensive decision making due to the number of criteria including.

- Population size and traits,
- The competition,
- Transportation access,
- Parking availability,
- The nature of nearby stores,
- Property costs,
- The length of the agreement,
- Legal restrictions and
- Other factors.

A store location may necessitate a sizable investment and a long term commitment. The Retailers moving from one location to another faces three potential problems.

(1) Some loyal customers and employees may be lost; the greater the distance between the old and new sites, the bigger is the loss.

(2) A new site may not have the same traits as the original one.

(3) Store fixtures and renovations at an old site usually cannot be transferred to a new site; their remaining value is lost if they have not been fully depreciated.

Location decision involves two different factors namely **cost factor** and **revenue factor.**

Location is a major **cost factor** because it

- involves large capital investment
- affects transportation costs
- affects human resources cost e.g., salaries

Location is a major **revenue factor** because it

- affects the amount of customer traffic
- affects the volume of business

FACTORS INFLUENCING RETAILER'S CHOICE OF LOCATION

Decisions regarding the location of a store are very critical not only to the future performance of that outlet but also the retailer's long term prosperity. This is compounded by the consideration of certain specific issues such as:

- **Consumer's Choice**: The consumer behavior is most often guided by their consideration of the ideal location to shop
- **To Gain Competitive Advantage**: The decision on where to locate the retail outlet will be of strategic importance because if they develop the best location, it will earn them a long term competitive advantage.
- **Understanding of the Structural and Social Changes:** Any decision on location will definitely have to take into consideration the existing trends and likely social changes.
- **High Investment Involving long term Financial Implications**: The retailer has to consider the investment cost, lead times and long term financial implications involved in the development of a retail location and site.
- **Government Formalities:** There could be many government policy decisions having a binding on the development of new retail outlets. This implies there could be restrictions on selection of new location sites for retailing purposes.

LEVELS OF LOCATION DECISIONS AND ITS DETERMINING FACTORS

A retailer has to take the location decision, basing on three aspects:

(1) Selection of a city

(2) Selection of an area or type of location within a city

(3) Identification of a specific site

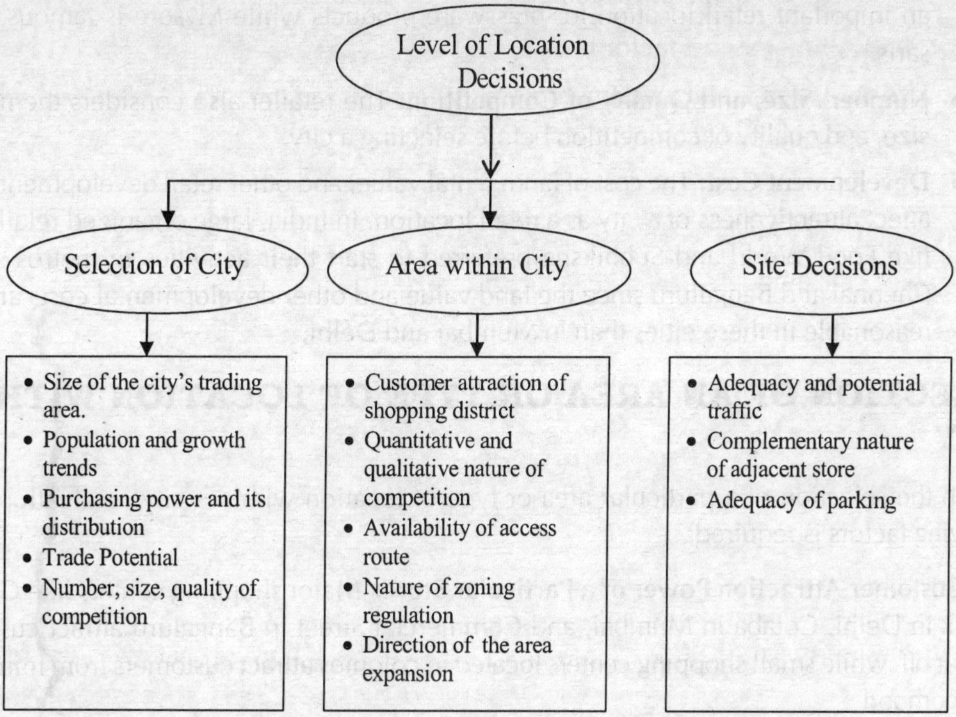

Figure 1

The factors which influence these decisions are discussed in the following sections.

SELECTION OF A CITY

The following factors play a significant role in the selection of a particular city for starting or relocating an existing retail business

- **Size of the City's Trading Area:** A city's trading area is the geographic region from which customers come to the city for shopping. A city's trading area would comprise its suburbs as well as neighboring cities and towns. Cities like Mumbai and Delhi have a large trading area as they draw customers from far off cities and towns.
- **Population or Population Growth in the Trading Area:** The larger the population of the trading area, the greater the potential of the city as a shopping location. A high growth in population in the trading area can also increase the retail potential.
- **Total Purchasing Power and its Distribution:** The retail potential of a city depends on the purchasing power of the customers and its distribution networks in its trading area. Cities with a large population of affluent and upper middle class customers can be an attractive location for stores selling high priced products.
- **Total Retail Trade Potential for Different Lines of Trade:** A city may become specialized in certain lines of trade and attract customers from other cities. Moradabad has become

an important retail location for brassware products while Mysore is famous for silk saris.

- **Number, Size, and Quality of Competition:** The retailer also considers the number, size, and quality of competition before selecting a city.
- **Development Cost:** The cost of land, rental value, and other retail developmental costs affect attractiveness of a city as a retail location. In India, large organized retail chains like Food World and Subhiksha preferred to start their activities in metros such as Chennai and Bangaluru since the land value and other developmental costs are more reasonable in these cities than in Mumbai and Delhi.

SELECTION OF AN AREA OR TYPE OF LOCATION WITHIN A CITY

In the selection of a particular area or type of location within a city, evaluation of the following factors is required.

Customer Attraction Power of a Particular Store: Major shopping centers like Chandni Chowk in Delhi, Colaba in Mumbai, and Commercial Street in Bangaluru attract customers from far off, while small shopping centers located in colonies attract customers from immediate neighborhood.

Quantitative and Qualitative Nature of Competitive Stores: Retailers would like to evaluate the product lines carried by other stores, number of stores in the area, *etc.* before selecting the area. Thus, Nai Sarak in Delhi would be a suitable location for retailing paper and stationery products since it has become a specialized market for these products.

Availability of Access Routes: The area should provide easy access routes. There should not be traffic jams and congestion. MG Road in Bangaluru provides easy access from different parts of the city and hence, has become popular.

Nature of Zoning Regulations: The retailer should consider the zoning regulations in the city. They should examine the plans of zoning commissions and municipal corporations regarding the development of shopping centers, residential areas, flyovers, *etc.*

Direction of Spread of the City: The retailer should consider the direction in which the city is developing while selecting the location. For example, Mumbai's suburbs and Navi Mumbai are growing at a fast rate. Gurgaon to the south of Delhi has similarly grown into an attractive retail location.

SELECTION OF A SPECIFIC SITE

The choice of a specific site is particularly important. In central and secondary shopping centers non anchor stores depend on customers coming to the market and the traffic generated by anchor stores. Large stores in turn depend on attracting customers from the existing flow of traffic. Where sales depend on nearby settlements, selecting the trading area is even more important than picking the specific site. The following factors need to be considered while selecting a specific site.

Adequacy and Potential of Traffic Passing the Site: The volume of vehicular traffic and pedestrian shoppers who pass by the specific site should be assessed since they represent the potential customers.

Ability of the Site to Intercept the Traffic Flowing Past the Site: The vehicular or pedestrian traffic moving past the site would be attracted only if it represents the segment the store is targeting. The presence of other shopping centers or stores in the vicinity can also influence the ability of the site to attract the flowing traffic.

Complementary Nature of Adjacent Stores: The site will have greater potential if the adjacent stores sell complementary products. Thus a store selling school uniforms would have greater potential if adjacent stores sell school books, stationery, *etc.*

Adequate Parking: Before finalizing a site it should be ensured that there are adequate parking facilities available in the vicinity, especially if the store expects substantial vehicular traffic.

TYPES OF LOCATION SITE AND RETAIL

Solitary Site

This may be a single free standing retail outlet away from other retailers and positioned on a road.

The advantage of a solitary site are

- lack of competition,
- low rentals,
- lower operating costs which can be passed on to the customers,
- more visible since it stands alone and away from mad traffic rush and
- ease the parking problem.

The disadvantages are

- difficult to attract initial/new customers and
- promotional costs may be higher.

Such a location site may be operated by convenience shops, garages, discount warehouses or small eating outlet.

Unplanned Shopping Area Site

This may be a retail location where two or more outlets are in close proximity to each other. This type of location site may come into existence when a number of buildings have been converted for retail purpose. With many of the cities and towns going for extensions, many such central shopping areas or complexes or unplanned small shopping areas have come up.

The advantages of such outlets are

- Better accessibility to public transport vehicles and
- Convenience of saving time by shopping at a single location area.

The disadvantages are

- parking woes and traffic congestion,
- organizing deliveries,
- high rentals and taxes and
- difficulties in recruiting and retaining staff.

Planned Shopping Area Site

These types of retail location is usually architecturally designed and planned to provide a unique theme for a number of complementary outlets. It typically has a amalgam of different retailers to reflect the added diversity and interest. Normally, there will be balance in the types of stores represented and complementing other central retail business on the quality and types of goods sold by them. Generally such planned shopping areas are holistically managed and marketed.

The benefits of such planned shopping areas include

- balance and comprehensiveness of the retail offers
- more variety
- freedom for customers to shop in style
- ability to increase security
- reduce theft and
- adequate parking space for customers

The disadvantages will be

- inflexibility associated with the rental agreement and
- restrictions on the types of merchandise to be sold

The smaller stores may not be as successful as the established ones and there is a constant need to upgrade.

TYPES OF CONSUMER GOODS AND LOCATION DECISIONS

Another factor that affects site selection is the customers' perception of the goods sold by a store. Consumer goods are generally grouped into three major categories: convenience, shopping, and specialty goods.

Convenience Goods

Convenience goods usually imply products that carry a low unit price are purchased frequently. They involve little selling effort and are bought by habit. They are sold in numerous outlets. Products like candy bars, cigarettes, and milk are generally categorized as convenience goods. For stores handling convenience goods, the quantity of traffic is the most important. Convenience stores located in central business districts have the following benefits.

- Low prices and
- Have limited ability to generate their own traffic.

Convenience goods are often purchased on impulse in easily accessible stores in the neighborhood.

Shopping Goods

Shopping goods usually imply products with a high unit price. They are purchased infrequently and involve more intensive selling effort on the part of the store owner. Price, quality, and features of such products are compared across stores by customers. Shopping products are often sold in only selected franchised outlets. Examples of such products are men's suits, automobiles, and furniture.

For stores handling shopping goods, the quality of the traffic is more important. While convenience goods are purchased by nearly everyone, shopping goods are purchased by only certain segments of shoppers.

Speciality Goods

Speciality goods usually imply products with high unit price which are bought infrequently, which require a special effort on the part of the customer to make the purchase, for which no substitutes are considered, and which are generally sold in exclusively franchised outlets. Examples of such products are precious jewellery, expensive perfume, fine furs, and so on.

Speciality goods are often sought by customers who are already 'sold' on the product, brand, or both. Stores catering to this types of consumer may use isolated locations because they generate their own consumer traffic. Stores carrying speciality goods that are complementary to certain other kinds of shopping goods may desire to locate close to the shopping goods stores.

RETAIL LOCATION STRATEGIES

Choice of wrong location for a store will not only result in the retailer losing a great deal of business but it can also result in waste of money invested in acquiring the location building and shop fittings. Thus, depending upon the social and demographic changes affecting their customers, they should adopt a suitable retail location strategy.

There are other factors like location's accessibility and proximity to public transport terminus, facility for parking vehicles, variety of goods, competition, and costs, *etc.*, which play a decisive role in the customers' preference for the retail location.

Location strategies for certain types of retailers

Departmental Stores

Departmental stores are usually located in central business location and shopping centre areas. They are able to attract a large number of people due to their large size and merchandise. The departmental store can also create its own traffic for a shopping mall. This is because now many malls in India are planning to have the makings of a multi activity centre, with multiplex screening movies, fully air conditioned, good food, enclosed space during rains and parking facilities as an added bonus. Further, many malls design their tenant mix so as to attract certain type of customers who would prefer to shop at their speciality stores. Some malls and retailers are using the sharing and shining concept for retailing.

Speciality Apparel Stores

Speciality Apparel Stores thrive in most types of malls, lifestyle shopping complexes, regional shopping centers and speciality centers. Such location sites are preferred because they are capable of drawing large number of potential customers. They also provide entertainment and recreational facilities. Added to this, the shopping centres also provide security, long open hours, protection from weather and a balanced tenant mix to a match the target market's requirement.

Especially in case of apparels, shoppers prefer to compare alternative brands and spend considerable time on this. Since malls and such shopping centers facilitate this type of consumers' shopping behaviour, customers prefer such a type of location.

Category Specialists

Category specialists sell various products through its retail formats. Their choice of location is based on reasons such as:

1. These stores compete on price and these locations cost less than malls
2. Facilitates easy accessibility to parking spaces as the merchandise may be large and difficult to carry.
3. These stores act as a single destination store for selection, presentation, pricing, *etc.*, for the customer.

Grocery Stores/Food Stores

Grocery and food stores are typically located in strip centers. These grocery/food stores are price competitive and strip centers have relatively less expensive rent. People prefer to purchase grocery and food from such stores which carry convenience goods. Consumers are not willing to travel long distances for and put in more effort to evaluate goods prior to their purchase. Instead they would prefer to purchase grocery and food at such stores which offer quality products at reasonable prices. Of course, ultimately while selecting a location for the retail outlet; the retailer must evaluate the trade-off between the cost of the location against its value to customers, the type of merchandise being sold and the profit.

Questions

I. Fill in the Blanks

1. ________ may be a single free standing retail outlet away from other retailers.
2. ________ may be a retail location where two or more outlets are in close proximity to each other.
3. ________ usually implies products that carry a low unit price are purchased frequently.
4. ________ sell various products through its retail formats.
5. ________ are usually located in central business location.

Answers

1. Solitary site 2. Unplanned shopping area site 3. Convenience goods
4. Category specialists 5. Departmental stores

II. Choose the Best Answer

1. ________ goods usually imply products that carry a low unit price.
   (a) Shopping (b) Speciality (c) Convenience (d) Luxury
2. ________ is a single free retail outlet away from other retailers and positioned on a road.
   (a) Planned shopping area (b) Unplanned shopping area
   (c) Solitary site (d) Retail Malls
3. ________ usually imply products that are purchased infrequently and involve more intensive selling effort on the part of the store owner.
   (a) Convenience (b) Shopping (c) Speciality (d) durable
4. Grocery and food stores are typically located in ________.
   (a) Planned shopping area (b) strip centre
   (c) solitary site (d) unplanned shopping area
5. ________ sell various products through its retail formats.
   (a) Departmental stores (b) Speciality apparel stores
   (c) Category specialist (d) Grocery stores

Answers

1. c 2. c 3. b 4. b 5. c

III. Answer in One Word

1. What do you mean by solitary site?
2. What is meant by shopping goods?
3. What do you mean by grocery stores?
4. What is meant by speciality apparel stores?
5. State the difference between planned and unplanned area site

IV. Essay Questions

1. Explain the factors determining the location of a retail store.
2. Discuss in detail different aspects of location decisions.
3. Describe various types of location site.
4. Explain the factors determining the selection of a particular city for starting or relocating retail business.
5. Discuss various types of consumer goods.

Chapter 6

RETAIL ORGANISATION

INTRODUCTION

The term retail organization refers to the basic format or structure of a retail business designed to cater to the needs of the end customer. Through a retail organization, a firm structures and assigns tasks (functions), policies, resources, authority, responsibilities, and rewards efficiently and effectively satisfy the needs of the target market, employees, and management. As a rule, a firm cannot survive unless its organization structure satisfies the target market. Although many retailers do similar tasks or functions, there are many ways of organizing to perform these functions. The process of setting up a retail organization is outlined in figure.

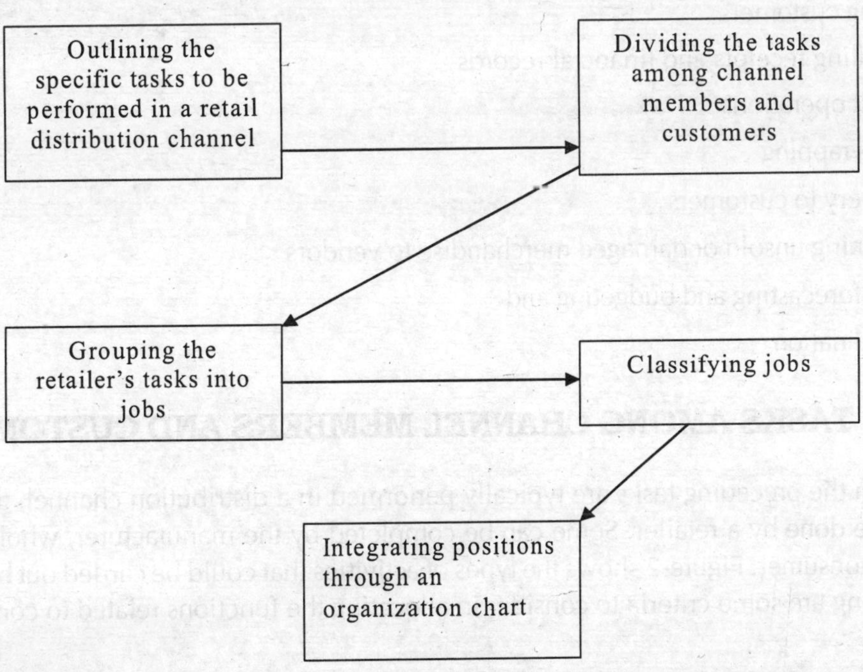

Figure 1

SPECIFYING TASKS TO BE PERFORMED

The tasks in a distribution channel must be enumerated and then keyed to the chosen strategy mix, for effective retailing to occur:

- Buying merchandise for the retailers
- Shipping merchandise to the retailers
- Receiving merchandise and checking incoming shipments
- Setting prices
- Marketing merchandise
- Inventory storage and control
- Preparing merchandise and window displays
- Facilities maintenance (e.g., keeping the store clean)
- Customer research and exchanging information
- Customer contact
- Facilitating shopping
- Customer follow up and complaint handling
- Personnel management
- Repairs and alteration of merchandise
- Billing customers
- Handling receipts and financial records
- Credit operations
- Gift wrapping
- Delivery to customers
- Returning unsold or damaged merchandise to vendors
- Sales forecasting and budgeting and
- Coordination

DIVIDING TASKS AMONG CHANNEL MEMBERS AND CUSTOMERS

Although the preceding tasks are typically performed in a distribution channel, they do not have to be done by a retailer. Some can be completed by the manufacturer, wholesaler, specialist, or consumer. Figure-2 shows the types of activities that could be carried out by each party. Following are some criteria to consider in allocating the functions related to consumer credit.

Performer	Tasks
Retailer	Can perform all or some of the tasks in the distribution channel, from buying merchandise to coordination
Manufacturer	Can take care of few functions, such as shipping, marking merchandise, inventory storage, displays research etc.
Specialist(s)	Can undertake a particular task: buying office, delivery firm, warehouse, marketing research firm ad agency, accountant, credit bureau, computer service firm.
Consumer	Can be responsible for delivery, credit, sales effort, product alterations etc.

Figure 2

A task should be done by the party with the best competence. Credit collection may require a legal staff and computerized records. Smaller retailers are likely to rely on bank credit cards. Task allocation depends on the savings gained by sharing or shifting tasks.

GROUPING TASKS INTO JOBS

After the retailer decides which tasks to perform, they are grouped into jobs. The jobs must be clearly structured. Here are examples of grouping tasks into jobs:

Tasks	Jobs
Displaying merchandise, customer contact, gift wrapping, customer follow up	Sales personnel
Entering transaction data, handling cash and credit purchases, gift wrapping	Cashier(s)
Receiving merchandise, checking incoming shipments, marking merchandise, inventory storage and control, returning merchandise to vendors	Inventory personnel
Window dressing, interior display set ups, use of mobile displays	Display personnel
Billing customers, credit operations, customer research	Credit personnel
Merchandise repairs and alterations, resolution of complaints, customer research	Customer service personnel
Cleaning store, replacing old fixtures	Janitorial personnel
Personnel management, sales forecasting, budgeting, pricing, coordinating tasks	Management personnel

Figure 3

While grouping tasks into jobs, specialization should be considered, so each employee is responsible for a limited range of functions. Specialization has the advantages of clearly defined tasks, greater expertise, reduced training and hiring personnel with narrow education and experience. Once the tasks are grouped, job descriptions are constructed. These outline the job titles, objectives, duties, and responsibilities for every position. They are used as a hiring, supervision and evaluation tool.

CLASSIFYING JOBS

Jobs are then broadly grouped into functional, product, geographic, or combination classifications. Functional classification divides jobs by task – such as sales promotion, buying and store operations. Expert knowledge is utilized. Product classification divides jobs on a goods or service basis. A department store hires different personnel for clothing, furniture, appliances, and so forth. This classification recognizes the differences in personnel requirements for different products. Geographic classification is useful for chains operating in different areas. Employees are adapted to local conditions, and they are supervised by branch managers. Some firms, especially larger ones, use a combination classification.

DEVELOPING AN ORGANIZATION CHART

The format of a retail organization must be designed in an integrated and coordinated, way. Jobs must be defined and distinct. Interrelationships among positions must be clear.

The hierarchy of authority outlines the job interactions within a company by describing the reporting relationships amongst employees. Coordination and control are provided by this hierarchy.

Principles for Organizing a Retail Firm

An organization should show interest in its employees. Job rotation, promotion from within, participatory management, recognition, job enrichment, and so forth improve worker morale.

Employee turnover, lateness, and absenteeism should be monitored, as they may indicate personnel problems.

The line of authority should be traceable from the highest to the lowest positions. In this way, employees know to whom they report and who reports to them.

A subordinate should only report to one direct supervisor. This avoids the problem of workers receiving conflicting orders

There is a limit to the number of employees a manager can directly supervise.

A person responsible for a given objective needs the power to achieve it.

Although a supervisor can delegate authority, he or she is still responsible for subordinates.

The greater the number of organizational levels, the longer the time for communication to travel and the greater the coordination problems.

An organization has an informal structure aside from the formal organization chart. Informal relationships exercise power in the organization and may bypass formal relationships and procedures.

ORGANIZATION PATTERNS IN RETAILING

An independent retailer has a simple organization. It operates only one store, the owner manager usually supervises all employees, and workers have access to the owner manager if there are problems. In contrast, a chain must specify how tasks are delegated, coordinate multiple stores, and set common policies for employees. The organizational arrangements used by independent retailers, department stores, chain retailers, and diversified retailers are discussed.

Organisational Arrangements used by Small Independent Retailers

Small independents use uncomplicated arrangements with only two or three levels of personnel. The owner manager personally runs the firm and oversees workers. There are few employees, little specialization, and no branch units. This does not mean fewer activities must be performed, but that many tasks are performed relative to the number of workers. Each employee must allot part of his or her time to several duties.

Organizational Arrangements used by Departmental Stores

Many departmental stores continue to use organizational arrangements which divide all retail activities into four functional areas – merchandising, publicity, store management, and accounting and control:

1. **Merchandising** – buying, selling, stock planning and control, promotional planning.
2. **Publicity** – window and interior display, advertising, planning and executing promotional events, advertising research, public relations.
3. **Store Management** – merchandise care, customer services, buying store supplies and equipments, maintenance, operating activities, store and merchandise protection , employee training and compensation, workroom operations.
4. **Accounting and Control** – credit and collections, expense budgeting and control, inventory planning and control, record keeping.

These areas are organized by line and staff components. Thus, a controller and a publicity manager provide staff services to merchandisers, but within their disciplines, personnel are organized on a line basis.

Organisational Arrangements Used by Chain Retailers

Various chain retailers use a version of the equal store organization. Although chains' organizations may differ, they generally have these attributes.

- There are many functional divisions, such as sales promotion, merchandise managements, distribution, operations, real estate, personnel, and information systems.
- Overall authority is centralized. Store managers have selling responsibility.
- Many operations are standardized.
- An elaborate control system keeps management informed
- Some decentralization lets branches adapt to localities and increases store managers responsibilities.

CHANGING STRUCTURE OF RETAILING

All dynamic developments in retailing, from the birth of departmental stores in the last century to the recent emergence of warehouse clubs and hypermarkets, have been responses to a changing environment. Changing customer demand, new technologies, intense competition, and social changes create new opportunities. Technological advances, changing demographics, and shifts in consumer preferences and shopping expectations will bring undreamt of changes in the structure of the retail industry.

In fact, the retail business formats have been changing very fast, mainly due to technological influences. The internet and the web technologies have created a myriad of opportunities for the web based business model of retailing. This has created a competition of the retailer with its own self.

CLASSIFICATION OF RETAIL UNITS

Conceptual classification of a business unit provides the marketers with strategic guidelines, useful in the design of retailing strategy. Besides, retail businesses are extremely diverse, and there are quite a few types of retail units. Therefore, retail units are classified on multiple dimensions such as margin, turnover, size, types of product sold, nature of ownership, geographical locations, kind of customer interactions, level of services provided, etc.

Bases for Classification of Retail Units

Retail firms can be classified into various format types based on the following criteria:

- **Nature of Ownership:** The three basic legal forms of ownership are sole proprietorship, partnership, and limited liability company (private and public).
- **Operational Structure:** The retail operational structures can be classified into the following three types: the independent trader, the multiple or chain store, franchising and the consumer cooperative.
- **Length and Depth of Merchandise:** Retail units differentiate themselves on the basis of the range and variety of merchandise they maintain in their stores. Some retail businesses offer a wide range of goods. On the other hand, some deal only in a specific product category with a minimum range of merchandise within that product category.
- **Nature of Service:** With the growing emphasis of retailers on service mix in their entire retail mix, retailers are classified on the basis of level and kind of services extended by them to their customers. Many self service retailers are now looking at ways of gaining competitive advantage by adding new customer services.
- **Type of Pricing Policy:** some retailers choose to emphasize the low price rather than the service element of their retailing mix. Others choose to price their offerings above the competition, knowing that they will generate business on the basis of some other attribute such as convenient location, premium merchandise mix or distinctive image.

- **Type of Retail Location:** Under this, retailers are classified according to their store's geographical location. With the increasing cost of central business district centre sites, limited parking facility, and traffic congestion, many retailers have out of town locations, whilst others have preferred to locate in 'cluster' locations in downtown centers.
- **Methods of Customer Interaction:** Traditionally, most of the retail interactions or transactions have been conducted by face to face contact in retail stores. However, a significant number of retailers are generating retail sales by non store retailing operations such as mail order catalogues, telephone selling, vending machines, door to door selling, or mobile vendors.

VARIOUS RETAILING FORMATS

There are many different retail stores in India – convenience stores, super markets, hyper markets, department stores, brand stores, and discount store characterized by the variety of merchandise mix offered by respective retail format. The consumer can choose between different stores for different needs. Retail units, on account of variety of merchandise mix, can be classified as Departmental stores, Discount stores, Speciality stores and Hyper markets. The various retailing formats that are operating in India are dynamic in nature, develop and change according to the needs and requirements of the ultimate consumers.

Mom-and-pop Stores and Traditional Retail Stores

The small mom-and-pop stores and the traditional department stores, are finding the competition intense from the organized retailing formats. The small mom and pop stores commonly known as the kirana stores are the convenience stores which provide the highest level of convenience to the customers especially in terms of food and other essential items. They offer a limited assortment and variety of merchandise, usually charge higher price than the supermarkets. Normally it remains open for long hours and shoppers use it for buying fill-in merchandise and emergency purchase. Small independent stores, across product categories, is a very common retail format in India, particularly in small townships, but with the emergence of new retail formats they also undertaking large scale renovations to appeal and attract their target consumer segments Kirnas are growing only at 8% per cent per annum while the demand is increasing due to higher household incomes and rise in the spending attitude of the people. Growth of kirnas is restricted by their weak financial state and physical space constraints. Retail is growing at a rate of 15% per cent per annum. This is the reason why modern retailing is growing rapidly.

Departmental Stores

Departmental store is a retail establishment which specializes in selling a wide range of products. It is a large retail store organized into a number of departments, offering a broad variety and depth of merchandise. Usually, department stores are located within the planned shopping centers. It offers an extensive assortment of goods and services that are organized into separate departments for the purpose of efficient buying, assortment, promotion and above all, ease of shopping for the consumer. Such a format provides the greatest selection of any general merchandise and very often serves as the anchor store in a shopping mall or shopping centre. They usually sell products like apparel, furniture, appliances, electronics and additionally select other line of products such as paint, hardware, toiletries, cosmetics, jewelry, toys, photographic equipment and sports goods. In India the number of department stores is less as compared to the other formats such as supermarkets and discount stores. Over the last decade, department stores have suffered badly. In part, this is a result of changing shopping patterns and increased competition from discount stores. Shoppers' Stop is the first one to open a department store in the early1990s and currently operates 19 stores in 10 different cities in India. The main focus is on life style retailing and is divided into five departments such as apparel, accessories, home décor, gift ideas and other services. The leading fashion department stores in India are Globus, Lifestyle, Pantaloon, Shoppers' Stop, and Westside. All of them are multi product stores.

Many leading independent retailers of the cities and even new entrants are indicating preference for autonomous department stores. For example, Appeal, a leading fashion store in west Delhi and the Baniya store in Jammu offer a wide range of products such as gifts, dry fruits, sports material, apparel, home fashion, curtains, bed sheets, *etc.* Customers are free to move around the store unlike the traditional counter setups on India.

Various departments within the store have a designated selling space allocated to them, including a point of sales terminal to transact and record sales, and salespeople to assist customers. A majority of the departmental stores possess women's, men's, kids' fashion accessories and kitchenware and home fashion departments. Some departments, to provide convenience to their customers in the browsing and selection of merchandise, have further sections within the specific department on the account of attributes of the product category.

Departmental stores provide a distinctive shopping experience to customers on account of services extended along with core offerings and atmospherics of the retail store. Pricing of the offerings is relatively high due to trained sales staff, range of merchandise offered and services, and high capital investments. Departmental stores, generally, opt for centralized buying taking into consideration the preferences and tastes of the consumers. In case of multiplicity of departments within stores, each department carries out its own buying in accordance with the demand patterns of their customers. Some departmental stores deal only in specific product category on account of variety and brands available in particular product category.

Discount Stores

A discount store offers a wide variety of merchandise. However, the quality and price range of the product is a little different with limited service but with discounted price. Retailers offering a broad variety of merchandise mix, limited or no service and low prices are characterized by low margins, heavy advertising, low investments on fixtures, limited support from sales people, *etc.* Discount stores prefer shopping centers that provide space at lower rents as they attract customers from other adjoining stores in the shopping centre. They mainly focus on the lower and middle income consumers unlike the departmental stores which cater mostly to the higher income group. Wal-Mart, the largest retailer in the world is a discounter. Subhiksha, the Chennai based discount retail chain is leading discount stores in the country. Where once mom and pop and Department Stores dominated retail, now the giant discount retailers like Wal-Mart and Category Killers like The Sports Authority are at the top.

In India, the 'discount store' concept works with a difference. Indian consumers are price consciousness, interested in the best of the offerings. One needs to classify stores on the basis of perpetual discount stores, extent of discount, category wise discount, item/brand wise discount, GP based discount, general discount, loyalty discount, special discount, festival discount, stock clearance discount, and fixed amount discount. Vendor partnership is an essential element in the success of the operations. A store's operations and inventory management need to be very efficient and effective to keep the running expenditure under control. Display should be self explanatory to guide the customer in his buying decision. Price tags should be pasted depending on the commodity so that they are visible irrespective of the category of merchandise.

Category Killers

The Category Killers concept originated in USA. It is a kind of discount speciality store that offers less variety but deep assortment of merchandise. By offering deep assortment in a category at competitive low prices, Category specialists can "kill" that specific category of merchandise for other retailers. This format utilizes the self service approach. They use their purchasing power to negotiate low price, excellent terms and assured supply when items are scarce. They are the giant retailers that dominate one area of merchandise. They are able to buy filing cabinets, electronics goods, furniture, bathroom tiles or pet food in huge volumes and soare able to sell them at prices which even large competitors cannot match. The future of category killers is better than many of the general discounters. In India, these kinds of retail stores are not prevalent at this point of time. But there is scope for such kind of format. In India, Mega-Mart is one sort of Category Killers which sells apparel products.

Speciality Stores

They are limited line stores and offer a much different range of services than convenience stores. They specialize in a particular line of merchandise in which they have a large variety both in terms of width and depth of their respective product. These stores concentrate on one type of merchandise and offer it in a manner that makes it special. Speciality stores stress on one or a limited number of complementary product categories and extend a high level of service to their customers. They offer the customer a better selection and sales expertise in that category than would be provided by department or discount stores. Industrial experts predict growth in this segment particularly in home furnishing and home improvement. In India, the traditionally independent retailers in the specialized market centre operate in a particular product category, as these centers attract large crowds. Such specialized retail operations provide expertise, economies of scale, bargain, and image to the particular stores.

Recently, with the advent of organized retailing, many companies and retail chains have opted for this retail format such as furniture, durables, watches, etc. In particular, this kind of retail format appeals to lifestyle product categories such as apparel, watches, home fashions, and jewellers. The largest penetration of organized retail would possibly happen in this format in categories such as health and beauty, home improvement, and IT products.

Branded Store

These are the stores deal with a single brand merchandise. These formats are very commonly seen in apparel's retailing. They satisfy customers who are more brands conscious and loyal to their own brands. For example, Raymond's, a nation wide retail chain has 260 Raymond shops dealing in fabrics, apparels and accessories. Liberty in footwear is one of the leading branded stores of the country. Reebok in sport shoes is also one of the leading branded stores in India.

Malls

Shopping malls are not retail stores in the true sense of the term. In a mall, a large number of stores are located. The varieties of retailers that are located within them are usually quite different from each other. For example, a shopping mall may have a McDonalds outlet as well as popular departmental stores as its anchor store. In 1998, almost no malls were in India but today we have around 220 malls in our country.

Super Markets and Hyper Markets

The supermarkets largely concentrate on selling food related product and are considerably smaller in size as compared to hyper market. The supermarket offer relatively less assortments but focus on specific product categories. In India Food World, Food Bazaar, Nilgris are the leading super market operators.

A hypermarket is a very large retail unit offering merchandise at low prices. Super stores have a sales area of about 25,000 to 50,000 sq ft, while hyper markets have selling area of over 50,000 sq. ft. Hypermarkets are characterized by large store size, low operating costs and margins, low prices, and a comprehensive range of merchandise. Hypermarkets own spacious parking facility exclusively for their customers and employees. Hypermarkets not only offer consumers the largest merchandise mix, product and brand choice under one roof, but also create value for money. In India, hypermarkets are spread over 50,000 sq.ft. There are more than 25,000 Stock Keeping Units. Their product offering ranges from fresh produce and FMCG products to electronics, apparels, house-ware, *etc*. They combine supermarket and discount store retailing principles. The number of players operating the hypermarket format is increasing day by day in India. One of the leading players in this format is Pantaloon Retails India Limited which operate 32 big bazaars in 20 cities. Reliance is operating its own hypermarket under the caption " Reliance Mart". Hypermarkets are springing up all over India since consumers can buy groceries, food, garments, home appliances, durables, toys, cosmetics, toiletries, books, and music at a price that is lower than the market price by 5-50 per cent. Currently there are around 40 hypermarkets in India.

Hypermarkets are still at an experimental stage in India. The challenge ahead with marketers is to build themselves as service brands by integrating distinct consumer offerings and aggressive mass media campaigns as a core holistic strategy. In this regard, the hypermarkets need to demonstrate the concept of prolonged shopping as a functional mode of entertainment to the Indian consumers, to ensure the success of emerging retail format. Therefore, the success of hypermarkets depends on the transition the Indian consumer makes from activity based shopping to plan out leisure shopping.

RPG, a leading corporate house in organized retailing, decided to experiment with just one hypermarket, called 'Giant', which was set up in Hyderabad in June 2001. A separate company, Great Wholesale Club, was created for the ownership and management of the Giant chain. The first Giant was a 50,000 sq. ft site. It stocked over 20,000 products. While groceries accounted for about 60% of sales, the store also sold a large number of other products like consumer durables, garments, and luggage. At Giant one could get groceries, fresh fruit, vegetables, home appliances, white goods, luggage, and anything one wanted at discounted prices.

e-Tailing

It is selling of retail goods on the internet. It is the shortest form of electronic retailing. e-Tailing is considered as the fastest growing sector of the retail industry. In 2000, the share of e-Tailing was just 0.3% of the total retail business in India. This has given immense opportunity for most of the retailers to enter into this field. The development of e-Commerce infrastructure is indicating a trend in favour of e-Tailing. The internet users in India estimated to be four million are young and educated. The amount of retail business being conducted on the Internet is growing every year. Many major retail organisations and manufacturers have online retail stores. Major players like Amazon.Com have generated enough business to attract competitors to come up with their own internet sites. Traditional retailers like Wal-Mart who are successful in their own right have also set up online stores so as not to miss out the revenue opportunities that the internet offers. Pantaloon India Private limited is operating through Future Bazaar in e-Tailing segment along with Fab Mall and others.

Retailers usually provide merchandise and services to their customers. The mix of services and goods varies across the retail formats in retail industry according to the level of competition, store image, target segment, etc. Some retail formats have self service provision, with no assistance from sales force, in order to provide merchandise at low price. On the other hand, particular retail formats such as specialty stores and franchised outlets provide a set of multiples services, such as free home delivery, sales force, alterations, returns, and adjustments along with the core merchandise to the customers

METHODS OF CUSTOMER INTERACTION

Retail units can be classified into two groups on the basis of the nature of interaction between retailers and customers, namely store retailers and non store retailers. Retail transactions are carried out through face to face interaction between retailers and customers in the case of retail stores, whereas non store retailers sell to the customers in the absence of a retail store. Interactions between two entities take place without face to face interaction through Internet, TV, mail catalogue. Most of the non stores retailing media are well known on account of the medium used by them to interact with their customers.

Store Retailers

Store retailers operate from fixed point of sale locations to attract a high volume of walk in customers. Retail stores have extensive displays of merchandise and use mass media advertising to attract customers. They sell products and services to the customers for personal or household consumption, but some retailers also serve business and institutional clients such as office supplies stores, computer and software stores, gasoline stations, banks' branches building material dealers, and electrical supplies stores. In addition to selling products, some store retailers also provide after sales services, such as repair, alterations, and installation.

Non Store Retailers

Non store retailers approach their customers and market merchandise with methods such as the broadcasting of infomercials on TV channels, the broadcasting and publishing of direct response advertising, the publishing of traditional and electronic catalogues, door to door solicitation, in home demonstration, temporary displaying of merchandise and vending machines. The methods of transaction and delivery of merchandise vary across types of non store retailers. For example, non store retailers that reach their customers using information technologies can receive payment at the time of purchase or at the time of delivery, and the delivery of the merchandise may be done by the retailer or by a third party such as the post office or a courier. In contrast, non store retailers that reach their customers by door to door solicitation, in home demonstration, temporary displaying of their offerings and vending machines, receive payment and deliver the merchandise to the customer at the time of purchase.

Electronic Retailing

Electronic retailing has been acknowledged as one of the formidable non store retail formats in the retailing industry since the arrival of mail order retailing in the nineteenth century. E – Tailing is considered to be the fastest growing sector of the retail industry.

Internet retailing had a positive impact on the economy of the nation in particular and the world at large. In India, it will be a mixture of e-tailing and retailing that will work. Companies are working hard on reaching out to their consumers with the help of Internet. It helps prospective customers to acquire information about the offers or retailers at minimal cost in terms of traveling time and cost.

Internet retailing appeals to marketers and retailers on account of the following factors:

- Internet retailers can avoid expensive capital investment on stores and in store fittings, sales persons, and inventory holding costs.
- Internet retailers depend on IT integration from their store front to order processing all the way back to their suppliers. This will help to reduce the costs of acquiring and delivering throughout the value chain, which in turn help the marketers to share benefits with customers.
- Internet retailing widens the market to be served and provides national or international presence.

Catalogue and Direct Mail Retailing

It is a form of non store retailing in which retail units communicate about their merchandise or service through a catalogue. This retail format is new to Indian retail industry and is at a very nascent stage of its developments. Direct mail retailing is a non store retail format in which retailers communicate with their customers using mails/letters or brochures. Retailers directly mail advertising material to their existing or potential customers with the objective of selling goods or services.

Direct Selling

It is a retail format which involves personal contact between retailer and customers at any convenient place. It also includes the phone interactions between retailers and customers. The salesperson needs to demonstrate the product, to take orders, and to deliver the product selected by the consumer. This retail format is considered highly interactive in nature, which is compatible with retailing of the products high on information and search attributes such as jewellery, cosmetics, vacuum cleaner, etc.

Trends that have increased the use of direct marketing include:

- Increasing number of women in the workforce
- High costs of driving, including traffic congestion and parking problems.
- Shortage of retail help at retail stores limited or no help at self service stores
- Long checkout lines
- Toll free telephone numbers to place order or register complaints
- Availability of credit through proliferation of credit cards

- Growth of computer power and communication technology
- Increasing time pressure on consumer

Direct selling companies do away with wholesalers, retailers and other middlemen in the supply chain, thereby reducing their distribution and advertising costs. Direct selling has minimal support of advertising and large dependence on word of mouth publicity. There are certain strategic business advantages of direct selling. Some of them are as follows:

- Reduced cost for the seller
- Lower prices for the buyer
- Large geographical coverage
- Convenience for customers
- Ability to pin point customers segments
- Ability to supplement regular business without additional outlets

Television Shopping

It is a retail format in which existing and prospective customers watch a TV programme demonstrating products and then placing order for the same by telephone, email, and internet. There are three types of television shopping, namely cable channels meant for shopping, infomercials, and direct response advertising shown on TV. Infomercials are TV programmes that mix entertainment with product demonstrations and then interested customers place orders by telephone or email.

Vending Machine Retailing

It is a form of non store retailing in which products or services are placed in a machine and suspense to customers when they deposit cash or use plastic money (credit or debit card). Vending machines are found everywhere; compared to store retailing, vending machines offer consumers greater convenience 24 hours a day, and have replaced many services formally requiring a human interface. The expensive equipment and labor required to stock and service vending machines makes this a costly channel of distribution, and prices of vended goods are often 15 to 20% higher than those in retail stores.

Questions

I. Fill in the Blanks

1. __________ refers to the basic format of a retail business designed to cater to the needs of the end customer.
2. __________ stress on one or a limited number of complementary product categories.
3. __________ is a very large retail unit offering merchandise at low prices.
4. __________ is a non store retail format.
5. __________ is a retail format which involves a personal contact between retailers and customers at any convenient place.

Answers

1. Retail organization 2. Speciality stores 3. Hypermarket 4. Direct mail retailing

5. Direct selling

II. Choose the Best Answer

1. Retail __________ refers to the basic format of a retail business designed to cater to the needs of the customer.

   (a) layout (b)design (c)organisation (d)location

2. Sales forecasting, budgeting are the job of ________ personnel.

   (a)inventory (b) display (c) management (d) customer service

3. Retail formats are changing very fast mainly due to __________ influences

   (a)environmental (b)global (c)technological (d)social

4. In ________ stores broad variety of merchandise mix at low price with limited service is offered.

   (a) chain (b) discount (c) department (d) speciality

5. ____________ have selling area over 50,000 sq.ft.

   (a)Hypermarkets (b)Super market

   (c)Chain store (d)Departmental store

Answers

1.c 2.c 3.c 4.b 5.a

III. Answer in One sentence

1. What is Organisation Chart?
2. What do you mean by Speciality Stores?
3. What do you mean by hypermarkets?
4. What are discount stores?
5. What do you mean by electronic retailing?

IV. Essay Type Questions

1. Explain the process of setting retail organization
2. Discuss the organizational arrangements used by departmental stores
3. Describe the bases for classification of retail units
4. Discuss the Supermarkets and Hypermarkets
5. Describe the method of customer interaction in retailing.
6. Discuss the various retailing formats in India.

Chapter 7

RETAIL STORE LAYOUT AND DESIGN

INTRODUCTION

Atmospherics and retail space management are critical to any form of retail business. Their relevance emerges from the link between shopping behavior and physical environmental factors. Physical environmental factors influence the perception of shopping hours spent and the evaluation of merchandise. It, therefore, becomes important for the retailer to effectively plan and organize all the aspects related to atmospherics and retail space to be able to optimize scarce resources and improve profitability.

Atmospherics refers to the physical characteristics associated with the store. These characteristics include both interior and exterior elements, as well as layout planning and display. Display is popularly referred to as visual merchandising. Atmospherics plays a significant role in retail marketing. It attracts customers to the stores, improves the quality of service experience, creates a brand positioning for the outlet, and improves customer retention rates.

Another equally significant but related concept is retail space management. Effective space management attempts to ensure optimum utilization of retail space along with convenience to customers and employees. Today, the competition among the retailers is no longer restricted to the products/services they sell, but it is all about the total shopping experience offered to their customers. Right location, attractive and convenient store designs and layouts have become the prime considerations in the customers' retail store choice. Store location, store design, and store layout are the vital issues in the store retailing. They are the ingredients of store planning.

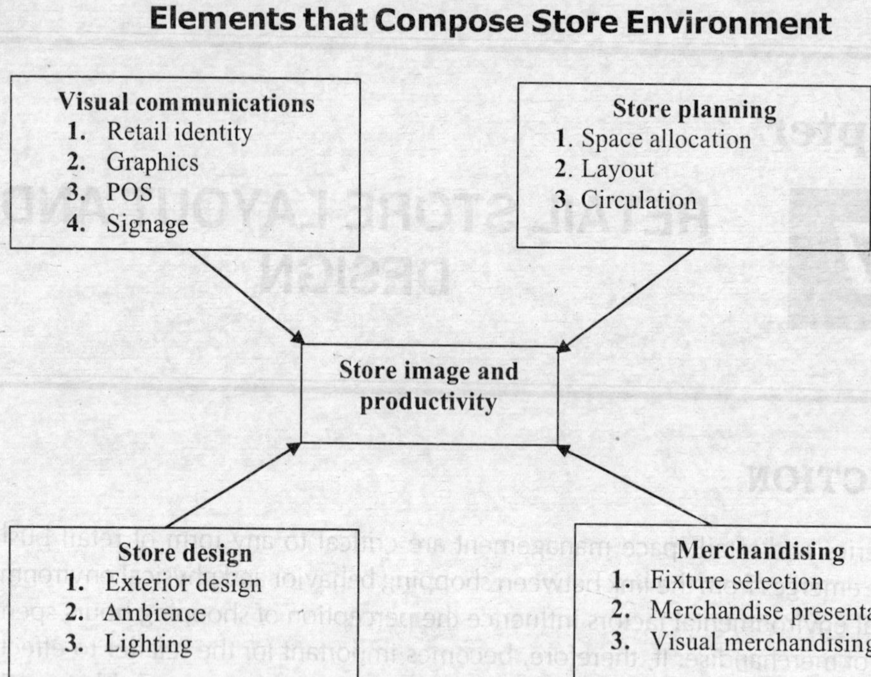

Figure 1

ELEMENTS OF THE STORE ENVIRONMENT

The first decision the retailer must make in planning a store is how to allocate the scarce resource, space. The retailer creates a store layout that shows the location of all merchandise departments. The merchandise presentation must be exciting so as to catch and hold customers attention, be easy to understand, and encourage shoppers to browse, evaluate, and buy. Therefore, the presentation of the merchandise is a critical factor in the selling power of a store. It has a significant effect on the store image. An effective store layout and design, including the storefront, creates a comfortable environment.

Lighting is an important element that should not be overlooked. Both display and in-store lighting help create the proper image and also draw customers' eyes around the store, onto merchandise, and ultimately encourage them to purchase the product. Likewise, in store graphics such as art, photography, and signs form an important visual communication link between the store and its customers. It provides much needed information on how to shop in the store.

STORE LAYOUT

Store layout refers to the interior retail store arrangement of departments or groupings of merchandise. It is important for retailers to evolve a customer friendly layout. This involves paying adequate attention to factors such as expected movement of the customers visiting the store and space allotted to customers to shop, and making adequate provision for merchandise display. These concerns are important as they contribute to the capital cost of the retail firm and also the overall image of the store.

The store can be said to be a product in its own right. The type of planned store layout can influence the customer's product decisions. Typically the store should be designed to facilitate the free movement of customers. It should create a planned store experience and also help to make an optimum presentation of merchandise. The retailer's goal while designing the store should be on a proactive basis – reflecting the brand position of the store. It should ensures most effective usage of the space.

The main objectives of a good store design should be:

1. The store design must complement the customers' needs, *i.e.*, be consistent with image and strategy.
2. The store design and layout should act positively on consumer behavior.
3. A good store design must consider the costs associated versus the value received in terms of higher sales and profits.
4. The store design should be flexible to adopt any changes in the merchandise with its image.

Store layout is much more than mere physical arrangement of the merchandise. It acts as an effective tool in creating a unique image of the store and attracting the customers towards the store. Layout should be designed considering the target audience of the outlet. It should consider customers' comfort and convenience in shopping. It should make them easy to move. There are many other factors, which influence the store layout.

Factors affecting store layout are as follows:

1. Total space available
2. Types of products offered by the store
3. Number of departments in the store
4. Volume and variety of product lines carried
5. Mode of operation, *i.e.*, whether the store is self service, sales staff assisted, *etc.*
6. Movement required in the store for locating, picking, storing the products.
7. Average number of customers visiting the store
8. Service requirements, size and location of service departments, facilities for the store employees, *etc.*
9. Degree of changes in the operations. The layout must be flexible and versatile
10. Inventory level. For example, the retailers who use automated order processing, follow supply chain maintain less inventory

TYPES OF STORE LAYOUT

In planning the layout, it is important to consider issues related to logical sequencing and category adjacency. The merchandise layout plan should be created according to the shopping habits of customers at the store. In this context, basics are items that the customers will seek. Seasonal items are products that have a limited shelf life. These can be placed up front, on power walls or high traffic areas. Impulse buys are best located in high traffic areas and around the case.

Store layout planning involves decisions about allocation of floor space, product groupings, and nature of traffic flow. It can take the form of:

- Straight or grid traffic flow
- Free form flow (curving)
- Racetrack flow and
- Storeyed layout to meet their specific requirements.

Grid Layout

In grid layout, traffic flow is in a straight line, this pattern is suitable when rectangular space is available. Supermarkets and food retailers use this pattern. Grid layout is cost effective as there is less wasted space. It is commonly used system followed by conventional grocery stores. It facilitates planned shopping behavior so that customers can easily locate product on their shopping list.

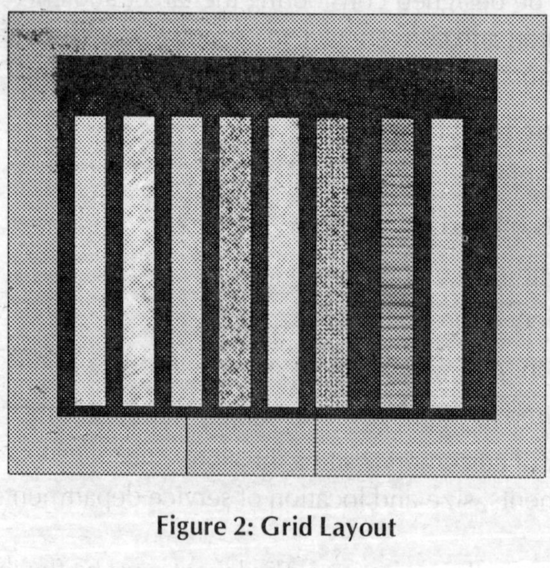

Figure 2: Grid Layout

This layout is comfortable for the shoppers who are frequent visitors. This reduces their search cost of locating merchandise in stores. Grid design is considered cost efficient by retailers in terms of space utilization. This design is considered to be the most space productive in terms of merchandise display. Grid layout saves expenditure on the fixtures, as it requires standard fixtures.

Free Flow Layout

This is simplest form. Free flow layout is also known as 'boutique layout'. Customers can move freely throughout the outlet.

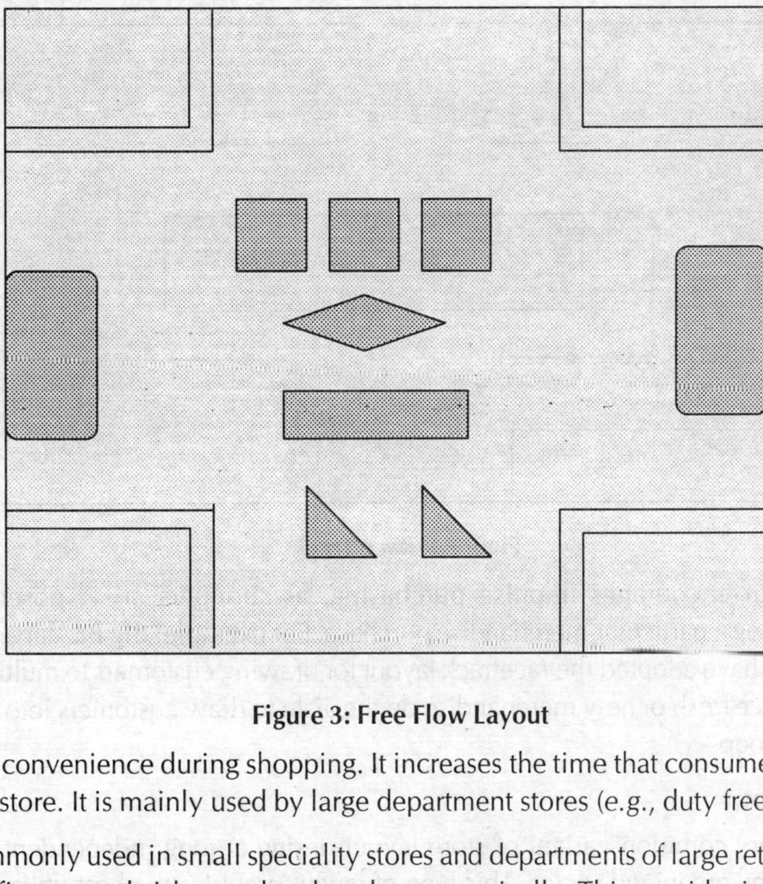

Figure 3: Free Flow Layout

It offers convenience during shopping. It increases the time that consumers are willing to spend in the store. It is mainly used by large department stores (e.g., duty free shops).

It is commonly used in small speciality stores and departments of large retail stores. In free form layout, fixtures and aisles can be placed asymmetrically. This provides informal setting to shoppers, which facilitates shopping and browsing.

Free form layout proves costlier in terms of high probability of thefts as sales people cannot manage simultaneously two adjacent sections or departments.

Race Track

It offers an unusual, interesting, and entertaining shopping experience. It increases impulse and promotional purchases. Customers visiting shops with this particular layout are required to navigate through specific paths. Therefore, visit to many store sections or departments are possible. They are exposed to a large number of products and promotional materials. Retail units with multiple departments opt for racetrack layout in order to attract shoppers to each department. It is also known as loop layout design. This layout encourages the customers to visit multiple departments. The customers can view the merchandise kept at both sides.

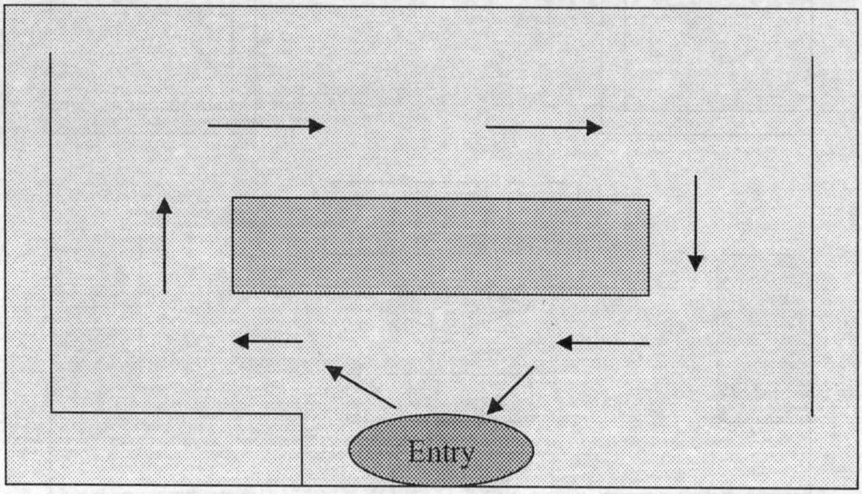

Figure 4: Race Track

Loop design encourages impulse purchasing, as shoppers are exposed to various departments during a particular merchandise purchase. For example, Big Bazaar and Pantaloon store in Gurgaon have adopted the racetrack layout for drawing customers to multiple sections. Departments place fresh or new merchandise on the aisle to draw customers into departments and around the loop.

Storeyed Layout

This is a very common variant of store layout design among independent and leading retail chains in the organized sector. This type of layout provides the best utilization of floor area. It also permits the retailer to set separate sections for different product categories. This arrangement provides comfort to the shoppers and also helps the retailers to manage the stock display effectively.

Storeyed layout is popular among the leading fashion department stores and supermarkets in India, such as Lifestyles, Shoppers' Stop, and Saravana. This kind of layout saves a substantial amount of initial investment of the retailer in a rising real estate cost scenario in the emerging retail market in India.

STORE DESIGN

Atmospherics is referred to as a store's physical characteristics that are used to develop the retail unit image and draw customers. It describes the physical elements in a store's design that appeals to consumer and encourages them to buy. Atmospherics can be classified in terms of exterior and interior atmospherics. Exterior atmospherics refers to aspects like store front, display windows, surrounding businesses, look of the shopping centre, *etc.* It is considered important to attract new customers. Interior atmospherics refers to aspects like lighting, colour, dressing room facilities, *etc.* It helps to enhance the display and provides customers with relevant information.

ROLE OF ATMOSPHERICS IN RETAIL STRATEGY

Atmospherics plays the following roles in the retail strategy:

- Enhances the image of the retail outlet
- Attracts new customers
- Generates excitement
- Facilitates easy movement inside the store
- Facilitates access to merchandise inside the store
- Ensures effective and desired presentation of the merchandise
- Reduces product search time for the customers
- Reinforces the marketing communication of the outlet
- Influences the service quality experience

Atmospherics is an integral part of the service quality experience for the customer and visitor to the retail site. Physical surroundings, in service setting are vital clues to service quality expectations. The choice of fixtures, décor, and signage can greatly alter consumer perceptions of a store. Effectively placed signs can help to reinforce customers in their role in service encounters.

KEY COMPONENTS OF RETAIL ATMOSPHERICS

Key components of atmospherics in the retail context are:

(1) Exterior atmospherics

(2) Interior atmospherics

Exterior Atmospherics

Exterior atmospherics refers to all aspects of physical environment found outside the store. It significantly affects store traffic and sales. Store's exterior is also referred as storefront. A store's exterior includes,

- Entrances
- Marquee
- Height
- Number of display windows and
- Uniqueness and visibility of store, *etc.*

The impact of store's exterior is also very important as it is the first part of a store seen by the consumers. This is the first impression that they carry when they enter the store. Then they look to the layout, displays, wall and floor, colors, lighting, kind of sales personnel that is overall store's atmosphere. This creates stores image in their mind. Many multinational retailers, chain retailers and franchisees are very much keen about storefront. Retailers always come out with some innovative techniques to enhance the store atmosphere to seek the attention of the customers as well as passive viewers. Storefront is an important decision criterion for the new shoppers in unknown retail markets.

Elements of Exterior Atmospherics

- Storefront
- Marquee
- Entrances
- Display windows
- Height of building
- Size of building
- Visibility
- Uniqueness
- Surrounding stores
- Surrounding area and
- Parking facilities

STORE FRONT

If the retail store can be compared to a book, then the storefront is like the book cover. It must be noticeable, easily identified by passing motorists or mall shoppers, and memorable. The storefront must clearly identify the name and general nature of the store. It should give some hint as to the merchandise inside. Generally, the storefront design includes all exterior signage and the architecture of the storefront itself. The storefront includes display windows, which serve as an advertising medium for the store.

Store windows must arrest the attention of passing shoppers, enticing them inside the store. Therefore, windows should be maintained with exciting visual displays. They have to be changed frequently and reflect the merchandise offering inside.

New age planned shopping centers and retail stores ensure accessibility to all customers, including those using wheel chairs. It should provide for the security of the store when it is closed. It is well researched that a wide opening for the store entrance is perceived as inviting by shoppers. Independent retailers prefer to have some pavement in front of their stores in order to place a part of their merchandise outside the store. This helps to draw attention and motivate shoppers to effect purchases.

Number of entrances is one of the important dimensions of retail store entrance decision. A small independent retail store usually prefers one entrance. In some cases, they have provisions of backdoor entrance used prominently for receiving fresh stocks. On the other hand, large department stores operate with four or more entrances to attract a large number of visitors in comparison to independent stores. These retail units have to make sufficient arrangement of entrances for vehicular traffic to their stores also.

Retailers have also to give due weightage to the kind of walkways with the store entrance. Indian stores have no or very limited provisions for customers to enter the stores. Traditional shopping district centers have no provisions of walkways for grocery or pharmaceutical stores. Customers are attended across the counters.

However, traditional independent stores such as garment or jewellery are characterized with wide open entrance with no walkways, enabling customers to step in directly. Walkways are important features of planned shopping centers which cater to high income sections of the market.

Display Windows

Display windows are very common features among retailers dealing in garments and gift items. This feature is even prevalent among retailers in small towns. Tall glass windows are common today in many retail outlets. They are used to display the store offerings and induce people to enter the store. In impulse buying, display windows play important role by tempting people to look at the products displayed. The customers can get idea about quality, prices of the products and outlet from the sample merchandise displayed in the windows. Display windows can attract the price conscious customers by showing sale items. It can get the attention of non price conscious customers by displaying unique, seasonal, or even offbeat items. Attractive displays make selling much easier and make the sales representatives' job easy.

Retailers can avail of the maximum benefits of window display only through a consistent policy not only while installing them but also in their day to day management. The relevant factors that retailers look into while deciding on various aspects of window display are number, size, shape, colour, theme of display, and the frequency of changes.

Sign Board/Marquee

A marquee is usually a painted or neon light displaying the store name alone. It may be mixed with trademark and other important information of a retail store at the storefront. In India, most independent retailers use painted tin boards placed outside the storefront. The quality of marquee influences the image of the store perceived by the customers. Most of the manufacturers sponsor marquee for the independent retailers with the name of the proprietor along with their own brand names and trademarks. Storefront and marquee play an important role in enhancing the visibility of the retail unit. It provides a clear view of the store to the pedestrian and moving vehicles.

Parking Facilities

Parking facilities play an important role in the success of a retail firm. The importance of parking facility is of great significance in urban shopping centers. Because the number of car owners is increasing day by day and people want to drive to shopping centers. Inadequate or absence of parking facilities may lead customers to go for the other alternatives. Thus, it may permanently take away the customers from the store. Retailers may lose the potential customers if they have to drive around looking for parking and spend their valuable time. Especially time poor customers are very keen on this aspect and they can debar such stores. Customers prefer the store that offers plenty, free and nearby parking facility. They can relax and enjoy their shopping more if they get convenient parking place where their vehicles are safe. Many retailers cannot afford to arrange for the ample parking space, due to high cost of land.

INTERIOR ATMOSPHERICS

Interior atmospherics refers to all aspect of the physical environment found inside the store. Interior atmospherics affects sales and time spends in the store. Point of purchase interaction and retail unit decoration influences the customers and in turn sales of the retail unit. The layout and design of a retail centre and store (e.g., traffic flow, allocation of floor space, layout of merchandise, passages, aisle, traffic patterns, *etc.*) have been found to affect unplanned purchases and perceptions of price value.

Interior design of stores is evolved by an intelligent combination of the following factors:

- Flooring
- Lighting

- Fixtures
- Temperature
- Colors
- Scents, sounds
- Wall textures
- Width of aisles
- Dressing facilities
- Dead areas
- Self service
- Prices (levels and displays)
- Technology/modernization
- Vertical transportation
- Personnel
- Merchandise
- Cash register placement
- Cleanliness

Lighting

Lighting arrangement adds significant meaning to the entire retail store atmosphere. The basic purpose of the lighting arrangement is that the shoppers can see the merchandise with ease. Retail setting looks brighter and more attractive to customers. Lighting affects the colour of the offering on display in the retail store. For example, garments and jewellery retailers use lighting to display their products better. As customers prefer to evaluate the colour, texture, and design of such offerings with ease, there is need for adequate lighting. Poor lighting will make them uncomfortable in determining the parameters of the offerings. This in turn can lead to loss of sale. Research findings indicate that blue colour light is preferred in case of stores selling toiletries and white in the case of medical stores.

Signage

Signages provide information regarding a store's policy in respect of returned goods, timing to return, prevailing discounts, *etc.* The type of signage used in terms of size. Lettering, and colors, and the placement of signage are indispensable parts of the entire retail unit designing.

Most of the independent retailers in India place such signage boards near the cash counters. Shoppers are found to place orders and make payments from this point of the store. For example, independent eating joints usually place the list of items available with their respective prices at the cash counters.

In respect of the large department stores and shopping centers, marketers have to work out a balance between providing all the information a customer is looking for and cluttering the place with too many signage boards. Retailers need to ensure that signages used in retail unit are complementary with the entire store design.

Music

Music is one of the key environmental variables that can influence shoppers. Environmental factors like music affect time spent in the store, propensity to shopping, and satisfaction with the shopping experience.

Visual Merchandising

Visual merchandising is defined as the presentation of products in order to sell them. The initial point of interaction with a potential customer is in the window displays of the storefront. Visual merchandising includes various aspects such as:

- Store floor plan
- Store windows
- Signs
- Merchandise display
- Space design
- Fixtures and hardwares.

Visual merchandising has been around since the dawn of civilization, when humans started selling merchandise to each others. When a retailer arranged his goods to be more attractive to a customer, or when a farmer put the best of his harvest on the top of the basket for the consumers to see and touch, that was visual merchandising. Visual merchandising has grown beyond mere arrangement of products for easy access to customers to a strategic issue in the retail management.

Visual merchandising is also known as a 'silent salesman'. Attractive displays silently invite customers to see and touch the goods. Visual merchandising techniques are put into practice right from designing floor plan of the store. With the speciality marketing of the 1990s, visual merchandising has become a necessity for the retail industry. It now envelops all aspects that go into creating and managing the overall visual presentation of the retail store environment. Specifically, it combines and integrates an understanding of merchandise presentation, display, and retail design. It is the art of presentation which brings the merchandise into focus. It is expected to educate the customers, create desire, and finally augment the shopping process.

Organizing the Display

Organizing a display involves planning for three key aspects

- Deciding on the display theme or concept
- Identifying locations for it and

- Selecting and determining the nature of various display components

Display concepts can be based on one or a combination of the following themes.

- Seasons
- Special occasions or holidays
- Colors
- Trends and activities (e.g., fishing, scrap booking, rangoli and collage, etc.)
- Themes (e.g., Victorian, children, ethnic, western, construction, etc.)
- Events of the community

There are many locations within a store where displays can be set up. Some of them are:

- Front windows
- Small platform at the entrance
- End caps
- Display or product cases (for particular types of merchandise such as jewellery)
- Behind the check out counter
- On counters
- Designated display areas

Components of Display

With a theme of the display determined and the location for it planned, the retailer needs to examine the components of the display. The various components of the display are as follows.

- Wall displays refer to slat wall panels and fixtures, grid wall panels and displays, slotted wall standards, face outs and shelving.
- Floor fixtures and grid wall panels and accessories, garment racks, display cases and counters, metal shelving gondolas, floor and cube merchandisers.
- Display products refer to mannequins and body forms, clear acrylic displays, and countertop and jewellery displays.
- Supplies and equipment include hangers and steamers, tagging supplies and labelers, packaging and shopping bags, *etc.*
- Promotional items include window signs and banners, sign holders and sign cards and sales tags and tickets.
- Lighting fixtures include track lighting and accessories such as rope lights. Lighting needs to come from more than one direction for a balanced presentation.
- Signage should be professional, never handwritten, regardless of the size. Bin tags, bin labels, peg tags, shelf labels and planogram tags are some others types of signages.

Shelf tags aid in the proper placement of product and frequently include price information for customers in lieu of price marking the individual items.

Factors to be Considered in Organizing an Effective Display

Factors like balance, rhythm, proportion, texture, harmony, and emphasis are important in organizing an effective display. The role of these factors and the techniques related to them are discussed below.

- **Balance**: It refers to an equality of optical weight and importance that creates a unified presentation. Balance could be of two kinds – formal and informal. Formal balance refers to symmetry. It is rigid and static but is simple and easy to use consistently. It helps keeps wall displays organized and maintains uniformity. Informal balance is asymmetrical. It uses optical weight to balance the display. There is greater freedom to express movement and activity.
- **Rhythm:** Lines can lend a rhythmic feeling to any display. Various line shapes can be used to create rhythmic effects. Vertical lines send a message of dignity, strength, and height. Diagonal lines speak of action, effective mood makers in sporting goods and toy departments. Horizontal lines are more restful and remind of landscapes. Curved lines are graceful, relaxed, and indicate carefree movement and a sense of femininity. Repetition also creates a sense of visual rhythm.
- **Proportion:** It refers to the relationship between the apparent sizes, mass, scale, or optical weight of two or more objects.
- **Texture:** Creating exciting and pleasing textures is important since people want to touch the merchandise. Texture can be both seen and felt.
- **Harmony:** It is important to build the display such that it is in harmony with the whole store. The retailer should keep the whole store image and merchandising goals in mind when building displays.
- **Emphasis**: Emphasis should always be on the merchandise. Emphasis could be through the use of colour, dramatic lighting, signage and graphics and strategic placements.

Benefits of Effective Displays

Displays and all visual merchandising techniques can communicate effectively with customers and can convert visitors, watchers, or viewers into buyers. They offer following benefits.

(1) Ensure maximum product exposure

(2) Inform, educate and entertain the customer about the services and merchandise offered by the outlet.

(3) Make it possible, accessible for the customers to see, touch or even try the merchandise.

(4) Enhance product appearance and create interest

(5) Emphasize on making right image of the store

(6) Encourage customers to enter the store and wander in store to discover more variety and novelty.

(7) Tempt customers to take quick purchase decision and impulse buying, thus, displays can generate additional sales through the impulse purchases

(8) Introduce new arrivals in store.

(9) Increased sales when there is a unique or special offer announced.

(10) Increase in store traffic and sales during low season or off season.

VISUAL MERCHANDISING IN INDIA

With the advent of foreign players and chain stores, independent retailers will have to compete purely on the basis of the competitive edge of the merchandise on display. Visual merchandise will be a helpful tool in projecting the uniqueness of the products. This will increase the market access and sales. It is high time the Indian retailers opted for some new age visual merchandise management in place of the traditional practice of display of merchandise. Still, majority of the retailers in the unorganized sector give limited importance to visual merchandise in the retail marketing mix.

Raymond's, the first men's garment retail chain in India, has always taken visual merchandising seriously. Their management has hired a professional agency for consistent and picture perfect window displays. They prefer a theme based merchandise display that does not involve the use of expensive raw materials. They feel that a theme based display provides the management with required flexibility and an opportunity to incorporate new ideas.

Questions

I. Fill in the Blanks

1. ________ refers to the physical characteristics associated with the store.
2. ________ refers to the interior retail store arrangement of departments or grouping of merchandise.
3. ________ is commonly used system followed by conventional grocery stores.
4. ________ is also known as boutique layout.
5. ________ offers an unusual, interesting and entertaining shopping experience.

Answer

1. Atmospherics 2. Store Layout 3. Grid layout

4. Free flow layout 5. Race track

II. Choose the Best Answer

1. __________ is popularly known as visual mechandising.
   (a) Display (b) Exhibition (c) Arrangement (d) Layout
2. Effective space management ensure__________ utilization of retail space.
   (a) minimum (b) maximum (c) optimum (d) normal
3. Stores _________ refers to the interior retail store ____ arrangement of departments.
   (a) location (b) layout (c) design (d) display
4. In __________ layout traffic flow is in a straight line.
   (a) free flow (b) racetrack (c) grid (d) storeyed
5. __________ layout is popular among leading fashion department stores.
   (a) Free flow (b) Race track (c) Grid (d) Storeyed
6. __________ should give some hint as to the merchandise inside.
   (a) Entrance (b) Surrounding area (c) Store front (d) Marquee

Answers:

1. a 2.c 3. b 4. c 5.d 6. c

III. Answer in One sentence

1. What is Atmospherics?
2. What do you mean by Store layout?
3. What is Grid layout?
4. What do you mean by Free flow layout?
5. What is Race track?

IV. Essay Type Questions

1. Explain the elements of store environment.
2. Discuss the main objectives of good store design.
3. Describe the factors affecting store layout.
4. Discuss different types of store layout.
5. Explain in detail about storeyed layout.

Chapter

8

RETAIL LOGISTICS

INTRODUCTION

Logistics is the total process of planning, implementing, and coordinating the physical movement of merchandise from manufacturer (wholesaler) to retailer to customer in timely, effective, and cost efficient manner possible. Logistics regards order processing and fulfillment, transportation, warehousing, customer service, and inventory management. If a logistics system works well, firms reduce stock outs, hold down inventories, and improve customer service.

RETAIL LOGISTICS

It is the organized process of managing the flow of merchandise from the source of supply to the consumer – from the producer/manufacturer, wholesaler/intermediary through to the warehouse, transport to the retail units until the merchandise is sold and delivered to the customer The retail logistics systems will include the following functions:

- Physical movement of goods
- Holding of these goods at stock keeping units
- Holding of stock in sufficient quantities to meet the demand from the end customer
- Management and administration of the distribution system.

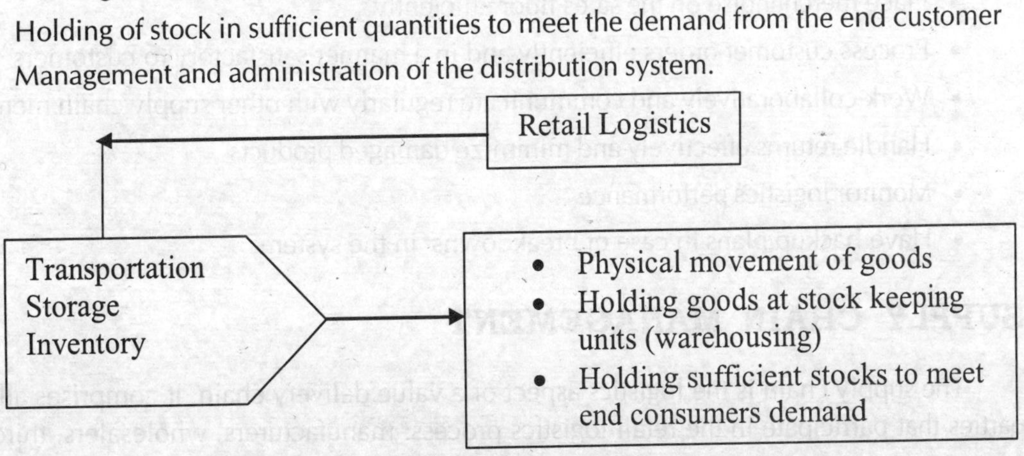

Figure 1

All retailer activity should be oriented to add value for the customer. So while trying to manage retail logistics, retailers have to work out on how activities are to be organized so as to take cost out of the supply chain completely as well as deliver better value for customers at the same time. Thus in today's market place, there are a few drivers for supply chain management.

- Consumers are having increased expectations of value addition. They are sensitive to response time, reliability, cost consciousness and information.
- Consumers are seeking retailers whose supply of merchandise ensures decreased lead times and costs
- There is a shift in the attitudes of retailers who are accepting the need for integration and sharing space and costs with complementary retailers.

Thus, Supply Chain Management (SCM)as an evolution from logistics management focuses on movement, storage and inventory issues.

In this section, logistics concepts: **performance goals, the supply chain order processing and fulfillment, transportation and warehousing, and customer transactions and customer service** are discussed.

Performance Goals

Retailers' major logistics goals are to

- Relate the costs incurred to specific logistics activities, thereby fulfilling all activities as economically as possible, given the firms' other performance objectives.
- Place and receive orders as easily, accurately and satisfactorily as possible
- Minimize the time between ordering and receiving merchandise
- Coordinate shipments from various suppliers
- Have enough merchandise on hand to satisfy customer demand
- Place merchandise on the sales floor efficiently
- Process customer orders efficiently and in a manner satisfactory to customers
- Work collaboratively and communicate regularly with other supply chain members
- Handle returns effectively and minimize damaged products
- Monitor logistics performance
- Have backup plans in case of breakdowns in the system

SUPPLY CHAIN MANAGEMENT

The supply chain is the logistics aspect of a value delivery chain. It comprises all of the parties that participate in the retail logistics process: manufacturers, wholesalers, third party specialists (shippers, order fulfillment houses, and so forth), and the retailer. Many retailers and suppliers are seeking closer logistical relationships; one technique for larger retailers is collaborative planning, forecasting, and replenishment. Retailers and manufacturers have different views of the market place. Retailers see and interact with the end consumer in person and infer consumer behavior. They also see a range of manufacturers, their product offerings, and their plans for marketing those products. Manufacturers see a range of retailers and their merchandising plans. They can also monitor consumer activity. The end result is a single shared forecast of consumer demand at the point of sale. A single demand plan can become the foundation for all internal planning activities related to that product for the retailer and manufacturer. It enables value chain integration.

ORDER PROCESSING AND FULFILMENT

To optimize order processing and fulfilment, many firms engage in quick response inventory planning. It enables a retailer to reduce the amount of inventory it holds by ordering more frequently and in lower quantity. For the retailer, a Quick Response (QR) system reduces inventory costs, minimizes the space required for storage, and lets the firm better match orders with market conditions – by replenishing stock more quickly. For the manufacturer, a QR system can also improve inventory turnover and better match supply and demand by giving the vendor the data to track actual sales. A QR system works best in conjunction with floor ready merchandise, lower minimum order sizes, properly formatted store fixtures, and electronic data interchange (EDI). Floor ready merchandise refers to items that are received at the store in condition to be put directly on display without any preparation by retail workers.

TRANSPORTATION AND WAREHOUSING

Several transportation decisions are necessary:

- How often will merchandise be shipped to the retailer?
- How will small order quantities be handled?
- What shipper will be used (the manufacturer, the retailer, or a third party specialist)?
- What transportation form will be used? Are multiple forms required?
- What are the special considerations for perishables and expensive merchandise?
- How often will special shipping arrangement be necessary?
- How are shipping terms negotiated with suppliers?
- What delivery options will be available for the retailers/customers?

This is the critical decision for nonstore retailers, especially those selling through the web.

Transportation effectiveness is influenced by the caliber of the logistics infrastructure. With regard to warehousing, some retailers focus on warehouses as central distribution centers.

The advantages of central warehousing are the efficiency in transportation and storage, mechanized processing of goods, improved security, efficient merchandise marking, ease of returns, and coordinated merchandise flow.

Key disadvantages are the excessive centralized control, extra handling of perishables, high costs for small retailers, and potential ordering delays. Centralized warehousing may also reduce the capability of QR systems.

CUSTOMER TRANSACTIONS AND CUSTOMER SERVICE

Retailers must plan for outbound logistics and inbound logistics completing transactions by turning over merchandise to customers. There are considerable differences between store based and nonstore retailers. Most retail stores expect the customer to take the purchase or to pick it up when it is ready. All direct marketers, including web retailers, are responsible for ensuring that products are delivered to the shopper's door or another convenient nearby location. Customer service expectations are very much affected by logistical effectiveness.

INVENTORY MANAGEMENT

As part of its logistics efforts, a retailer utilizes inventory management to acquire and maintain a proper merchandise assortment while ordering, shipping, handling, storing displaying and selling costs are kept in check. First, a retailer places an order based on a sales forecast or actual customer behavior. Both the number of items and their variety are requested in ordering. Order size and frequency depend on quantity discounts and inventory costs. Second, a supplier fills the order and sends merchandise to a warehouse or directly to the store(s). Third, the retailer receives products, makes items available for sale (by removing them from packing, marking prices and placing them on the sales floor), and completes customer transactions. Some transactions are not concluded until items are delivered to the customer. The cycle starts again when a retailer places another order. Various aspects of inventory management are retailer tasks, inventory levels, merchandise security, reverse logistics, and inventory analysis.

RETAILER TASKS

Due to the comprehensive nature of inventory management, and to be more cost effective, some retailers expect suppliers to perform more tasks or they outsource at least part of their inventory management activities; In 1990, producers shipped products to retailers in a warehouse ready mode. Retailers then reprocessed merchandise to package and price it for sale in the store where consumers make purchases. Today, in the era of floor ready, producers ship products that have already been packaged and prepared for immediate movement to the sales floor. As we move further into the new millennium, there will be a shift to consumer ready manufacturing where the links between producer and consumer are even more direct than traditionally.

INVENTORY LEVELS

Having the proper inventory on hand is a difficult balancing act:

- The retailer wants to be appealing and never lose a sale by being out of stock. Yet, it does not want to be "stuck" with excess merchandise that must be marked down drastically.
- Inventory levels must be planned in relation to the products involved: staples, assortment merchandise, fashion merchandise, fads, and best sellers.
- Customer demand is never completely predictable even for stables. Weather, special sales, and other factors can have an impact on the most stable items.

MERCHANDISE SECURITY

Retail sales are lost due to inventory shrinkage caused by employee theft, customer shoplifting, vendor fraud, and administrative errors. To reduce merchandise theft, there are three key points to consider:

1. Loss prevention measures should be included as stores are designed and built. The placement of entrances, dressing rooms, and delivery areas is critical.
2. A combination of security measures should be enacted, such as employee background checks, in-store guards, electronic security equipment, and merchandise tags.
3. Retailers must communicate the importance of loss prevention to employees, customers and vendors and the actions they will take to reduce losses.

When devising a merchandise security plan, a retailer must assess the plan's impact on its image, employee morale, shopper comfort, and vendor relations.

REVERSE LOGISTICS

The term reverse logistics encompasses all merchandise flows from the retailer back through the supply channel. It typically involves items returned because of damages, defects, or less than anticipated sales. To avoid channel conflicts, the conditions for reverse logistics should be specified in advance.

INVENTORY ANALYSIS

Inventory status and performance must be analyzed regularly to gauge the success of inventory management. Recent advances in computer software have made such analysis much more accurate and timely. Inventory turnover, gross profit percentage, gross margin return on inventory, the weeks of supply available, and the average in stock position are the various elements of inventory performance.

COST STRUCTURE IN RETAIL LOGISTICS

Everyone in the organization have to consider the components of distribution right from the manufacturer to the consumer through the retail outlet.

Total Distribution Costs for the supply chain will go by the formula:

TDC = TC + FC + CC + IC + HC + PC + MC

TDC = Total Distribution Cost

TC = Transport Cost

FC = Facilities Cost

CC = Communication Cost

IC = Inventory Cost

HC = Holding Cost

PC = Packaging Cost

MC = Management Cost

Thus the total distribution costs have to be considered in relation to each other and may also involve trade offs between service levels and quality or between margins and investment in systems. TDC permits retailers to exercise control over the costs as well as supply of goods to the consumers. But for this the retailer needs to have an understanding of the interaction of all the parts of the logistics process and then optimize the same. The above mentioned costs are briefly discussed hereunder:

Transport Cost

Transport cost structure includes substantial fixed cost elements with scope to adapt capacity to match volume. Centralizing retail distribution has led to improved efficiency due to the decrease in the number of journeys made with less than full loads. The use of composite distribution facilities enables the usage of the same vehicle to handle merchandise requiring different storage regimes – implying more frequent full load deliveries to stores.

Facilities Cost

Facilities cost includes the capital and running costs associated with providing warehousing infrastructure and internal systems to store and pick merchandise. Warehousing involves a high fixed cost element. There could be spare capacity which represents wasted resources and short term measures to cope with insufficient capacity. A regional distribution centre (RDC) is located in a low cost area and able to hold more stock in an efficient manner. Today usage of information technologies such as electronic data interchange, facilitates a reduction in stock holding in both store and distribution centre levels.

Communications Costs

These costs are mainly the administrative costs associated with order processing and electronic data interchange.

Handling Costs

These costs include the risk costs of damage and spoilage that could occur when merchandise or stock is moved through warehouse and transportation systems. Whenever an item is moved or stored, there is a possibility of damage, pilferage or deterioration. These will be treated as a part of handling costs.

Packaging Costs

These costs will be incurred by the retailer on all the materials used for packaging purpose. These costs would be through the use of pallet boards on which deliveries may be shipped and the use of shrink wrap or cling wrap film to secure pallets and roll cages during transit.

Management Costs

Management costs refer to all those costs which are incurred due to the control systems and mechanisms which are built into the retailers' logistics systems such as security systems, temperature monitoring systems and so on.

MERCHANDISE FLOWS

Logistics with reference to supply chain management is very comprehensive and strategic and includes customer relationship management, inventory management and vendor relations. When we talk of the physical flow of merchandise, it could flow from vendor to distribution centre (DC) to stores or alternatively the merchandise flows from vendor directly to stores.

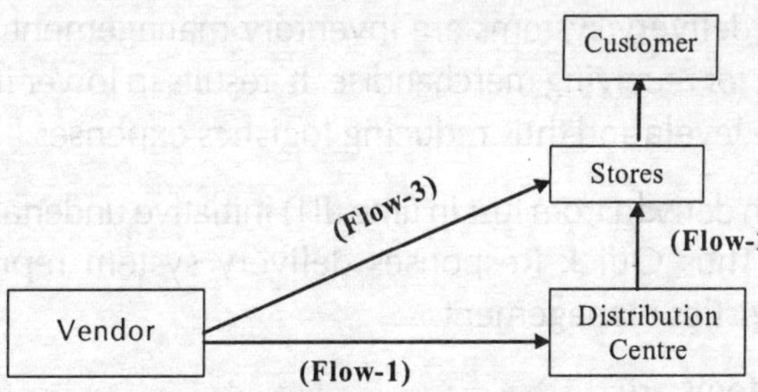

Figure 2

MERCHANDISE FLOWS IN SCM

We will start with the Flow 1, when merchandise flows from the vendor to the Distribution Center (DC). A usually carries out several functions which are given below:

- Management of transportation to facilitate merchandise flow from vendor to distribution centre
- Recording receipt of merchandise at the distribution centre and checking to ensure whether it is in order.
- Storing vendors may either store merchandise at the distribution centre or they may ship merchandise prepackaged in the quantity required at each store
- Getting merchandise floor ready, *i.e.*, ticketing, marking, labels showing price and identification marks, *etc.*

Thus, retailer can use either the push or pull logistics strategy. Push logistics strategy is a strategy in which merchandise is allocated to stores on the basis of historical demand, the inventory position at the distribution centre and the stores' need. Pull logistics strategy is in which orders for merchandise are generated at the store level on the basis of demand information or data obtained at the point of sale (PoS) terminals.

SPECIFIC LOGISTICS ISSUES IN RETAILING

Retailers are reacting to the competitive environment by changing the way they distribute merchandise. For this, retailers have to address certain specific issues in logistics. These can be broadly referred to as

a) Quick Response delivery systems,

b) Online logistics management or logistics of electronic retailing and

c) Outsourcing logistics functions.

Quick Response Delivery Systems

Quick Response (QR) delivery systems are inventory management systems designed to lower the retailer's lead time for receiving merchandise. It results in lower inventory investment, improving customer service levels and thus reducing logistics expenses.

The QR system has been derived from Just in time (JIT) initiative undertaken by manufacturers and adopted for retailing. Thus Quick Responses delivery system represents the nexus of information systems and logistics management.

The benefits of QR systems are

1. Lowers Lead Time: When vendors use computers for acquiring data electronically, no manual data entry is required at the recipient's end. This not only reduces the lead time but even manual data entry errors are eliminated. With a shorter lead time, it is easier to forecast demand and hence, the retailer needs fewer inventories.

2. Increases the Availability of Product and Lowers Inventory Investment for the Retailer: With using QR, the retailer can make purchase commitments closer to the time of sale for the customers. Thus retail stores may need fewer inventories as they are receiving less merchandise on each order. Thus the retailers' inventory investment is reduced and simultaneously product availability at the outlet also increases.

3. Enables Substantial Reduction in Logistics Expenses: When retailers use QR system they have got two options for reducing logistics expenses namely:

Use a Cross docking warehouse system which eliminates storage and some handling costs or use direct store delivery which eliminates all distribution centre costs and transportation cost from DC to stores.

Costs of a QR System

In spite of the many benefits of a QR system, it also involves the following costs:

- Greater order frequency involves smaller orders which are more expensive to transport
- It becomes more difficult to coordinate deliveries and transportation with greater order frequency
- Effectiveness of the QR system will require a strong commitment from the vendors' and retailers' side to cooperate, share data and develop systems such as EDI and CPFR.
- Successful implementation of QR systems requires financial support of the top management as well as psychological commitment to partners with their vendors.

OnLine Logistics Management or Logistics of Electronic Retailing

Logistics for fulfilling online or internet order is very different from distribution of merchandise to stores. Thus, retailers have to install a fully integrated information system which is able to handle properly the distribution of merchandise from Distribution Center (DC) to stores and to customers placing order via their website.

Outsourcing Logistical Operations to Third Parties

Outsourcing means obtaining a service from outside the organization; this in the past was done by the firm itself.

In order to streamline their operations and make more productive use of their personnel and assets, retailers sometimes prefer to outsource logistical functions. These outsourcing could be carried out in the following ways.

1. **Third Party Logistics Companies:** These are firms who will facilitate movement of merchandise from the manufacturer to retailer but are owned independently.
2. **Transportation Company:** Retailers may select transport companies carefully and demand reliable customized services and thus, help to reduce lead times.

3. **Third Party Warehousing:** In order to meet specific delivery times for floor ready merchandise, vendors may use public warehouses which are owned and operated by a third party.
4. **Freight Forwarders:** These are companies which consolidate small shipments from a number of shippers into large shipments which may charge a lower freight rate.
5. **Integrated Third Party Logistics Services:** This types of third party logistics providers are one stop shop providing transportation, warehousing and freight forwarding.

It is said that globally about 22 per cent of the organizations spend more than 10 per cent of their budgets on outsourcing. For instances, Tanishq has outsourced its web based supply chain development to Wipro Infotech.

Questions

I. Fill in the Blanks

1. ________ is the logistics aspect of a value delivery chain.
2. Retailer utilizes ________ to acquire and maintain a proper merchandise assortment.
3. In ________ producers shipped products to retailers in a warehouse ready mode.
4. TC + FC + CC + IC + HC + PC + MC is equal to ________.
5. Orders for merchandise are generated at the store level on the basis of demand information at the point of sales is called ________.

Answers

1. Supply Chain 2. inventory management 3. 1990
4. Total Distribution Cost (TDC) 5. pull logistics strategy

II. Choose the Best Answer

1. Retail ________ is the process of managing the flow of merchandise from the source of supply to the customer
   (a) organisation (b)logistics (c)merchandising (d) promotion
2. To optimize order processing and fulfillment, retailers engage in ________ inventory planning.
   (a) quick response (b) quite response (c) positive response (d) economic order response
3. ________ of inventory is caused by employees theft, customer shop lifting, vendor fraud and administrative errors.
   (a) Spoilage (b) Wastage (c) Damage (d) Shrinkage

4. Merchandise flow from retailer back through supply channel is _______ logistics.
   (a) downward (b) forward (c) reverse (d) upward
5. ___________ means obtaining a service from outside organization.
   (a) Electronic retailing (b) Outsourcing (c) Online logistic (d) Logistic

Answers

1. b 2.a 3. d 4.c 5. b

III. Answer in One Sentence

1. What is retail logistics?
2. What do you mean by supply chain management?
3. What is meant by merchandise security?
4. What is reverse logistics?
5. What is QR?

IV. Essay Questions

1. Explain the functions of retail logistics systems
2. Discuss major logistics goals of retailers
3. Explain the need for transportation
4. Describe in detail the cost structure in retail logistics
5. Explain the benefits of QR.

Chapter 9

SUPPLY CHAIN MANAGEMENT

INTRODUCTION

Supply Chain Management (SCM) is an end to end process in merchandise planning and movement, from planning the inventory (preparing the purchase order) to point of reaching the merchandise to the customers. SCM is an integrated process where every activity is interlinked with the system for information throughout the cycle time of each step of the process so that timely action can be taken.

MEANING OF SUPPLY CHAIN MANAGEMENT

The supply chain or distribution logistics encompasses all the activities and exchanges involved in extracting, processing, manufacturing and distributing goods and services from raw materials through to the end consumer. It also requires the retailers to take a holistic view of these activities and adopt innovative approaches to meet customer needs with great efficiency.

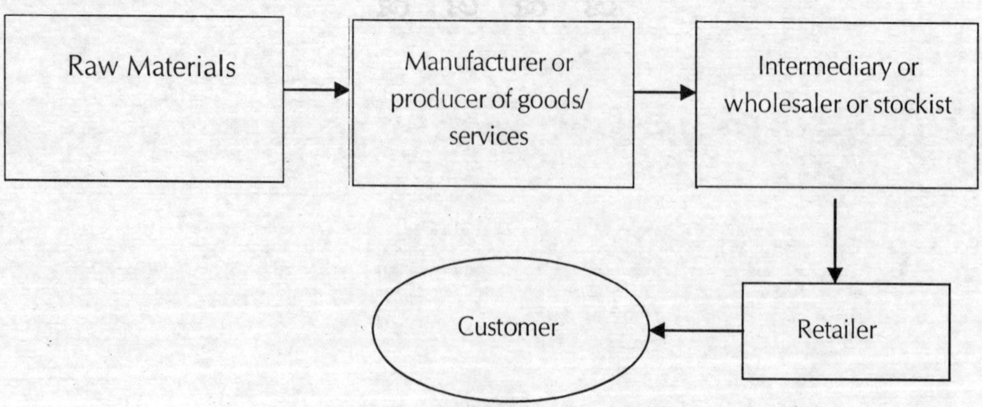

Figure 1

In the traditional distribution network, retailers sell merchandise which the manufacturer conceive and wholesalers supply. In this linear set up it was a left to right progression, wherein the customer stood passively, at the receiving end of the chain. But today, the consumer is more demanding and choosy because he is being wooed by many organized retailers who are putting all efforts to enhance customer value through establishing sophisticated logistics management systems.

Figure 1 indicates the various components in the traditional supply chain channel and the manufacturer, wholesaler and retailer have to build up a chain of facilitating services so as to ensure that the right product reaches the final customer. Here the manufacturer was dependent on the intermediaries to offer qualitative service throughout the chain, maintain low cost and then deliver goods and services to customers.

The supply chain, or channel, is affected by five external forces:

1. Consumer behavior,
2. Competition behavior,
3. Socio economic environment
4. Technological environment and
5. Legal and ethical environment.

These external forces cannot be completely controlled by the retailer or any other institution in the supply chain, but they need to be taken into account when retailers make decisions.

Eight marketing functions must be performed by a supply chain:

1. Buying
2. Storing
3. Selling
4. Transporting
5. Sorting
6. Financing
7. Information gathering and
8. Risk taking

Whether the economic system is capitalistic, socialistic, or somewhere in-between, every supply chain must perform these eight marketing functions. They cannot be eliminated. They can, however, be shifted or divided in differing ways among the different institutions and the consumer in the supply chain.

The institutions involved in performing the eight marketing functions are usually broken into two categories primary and facilitating.

Primary marketing institutions are supply chain members that take title to the goods.

Facilitating marketing institutions are those that do not actually take title but assist in the marketing process by specializing in the performance of certain functions. Figure 2 classifies the major institutions participating in the supply chain.

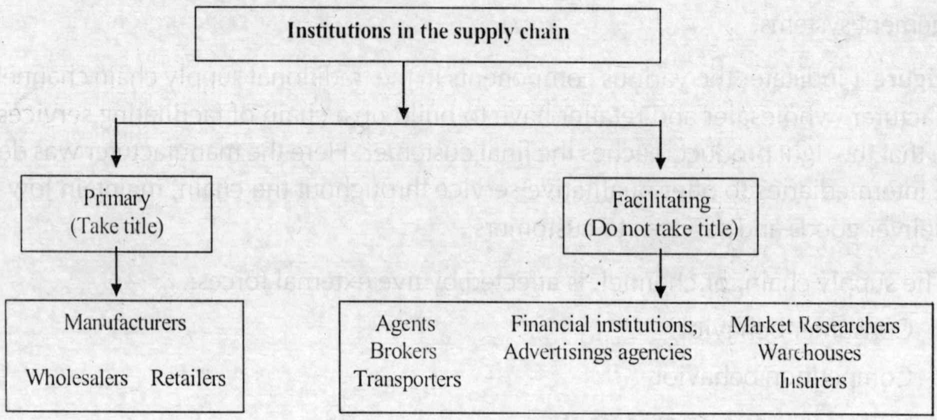

Figure 2

Primary Marketing Institutions

There are three types of primary marketing institutions: manufacturers, wholesalers, and retailers. Because they produce goods, we do not think of manufacturers as marketing institutions. But manufacturers cannot exist by only producing goods; they must also sell the goods produced. To produce those goods the manufacturers must purchase raw materials, semi-finished goods, and components. In addition, manufacturers often need the assistance of other institutions in performing the eight marketing functions.

A second type of primary marketing institution is the wholesaler. Wholesalers generally buy merchandise from manufacturers and resell to retailers, other merchants, industrial institutions and commercial users. The third type of primary institution is the retailers.

Facilitating Marketing Institutions

Many institutions facilitate the performance of the marketing functions. Most specialize in one or two functions; none of them takes title to the goods. Institutions that facilitate buying and selling the supply chain, include agents and brokers, who are independent business people. They receive a commission when they are able to bring a buyer and seller together to negotiate a transaction. Seldom do agents or brokers take physical possession of the merchandise. The purchasing agents assist in buying and the others assist in selling for manufacturers.

Marketing communications agencies, or advertising agencies, also facilitate the selling process by designing effective advertisements and advising management on where and when to place these advertisements. Institutions that facilitate the transportation function are motor, rail and air carriers and pipeline and shipping companies. These firms offer different advantages in terms of delivery, service, and cost. Generally, the quicker the delivery, the more costly it is. However, there is usually a trade-off because faster delivery enables the supply chain to have lower warehousing cost.

The major facilitating institution involved in storage is the public warehouse, which stores goods for safekeeping for any owner in return for a fee. Fees are usually based on cubic feet used per time period (month or day). Frequently, retailers take advantage of special promotional buys from manufacturers but have no storage facilities. As a result, they find it necessary to use public warehouses.

Other facilitating institutions in financing are commercial banks, merchant banks, stock and commodity exchanges, and venture capital firms. These institutions can provide the retailers with funds to finance marketing functions. Retailers frequently need short term loans for working capital requirements and long term loans for continued growth and expansion.

Finally, insurance firms can assume some of the risks in the channel. Insurance firms can insure inventories, buildings, trucks, equipments, fixtures, and other assets for the retailer and other primary marketing institutions. They can also insure against a variety of events such as employee and customer injuries, severe weather, changes in interest rates, and the impact of terrorist activity.

TYPES OF SUPPLY CHAINS

A large part of the supply chain consists of the marketing functions and the primary marketing institutions that perform them. There are actually three strategy decisions to be made when designing an efficient and competitive supply chain; supply chain length, width, and control.

SUPPLY CHAIN LENGTH

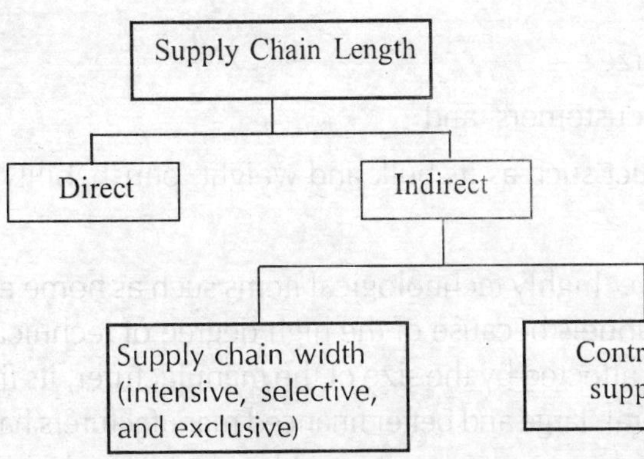

Figure 3

Supply chains can be direct or indirect. A direct supply chain occurs when manufacturers sell their goods directly to the final consumer. The supply chain becomes indirect once independent members are added between the manufacturer and the consumer. Indirect chains, may include just a retailer or both a retailer and a wholesaler.

Direct and Indirect Supply Chains

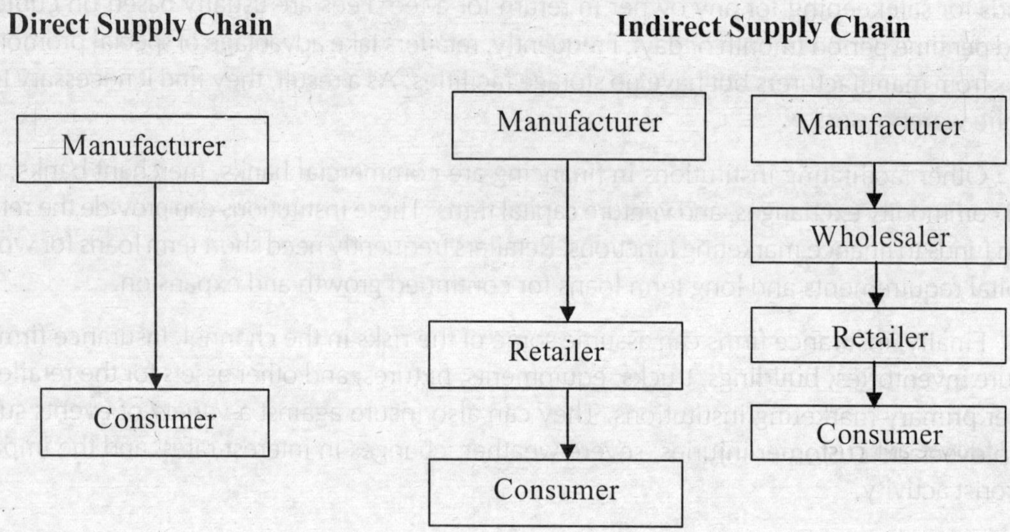

Figure 4

The desired length is determined by many customer based factors,

- Size of the customer base,
- Geographical dispersion,
- Behavior patterns
- Purchase frequency
- Average purchase size
- Particular needs of customers, and
- Nature of the product such as its bulk and weight, perishability, value and technical complexity,

For example, expensive, highly technological items such as home entertainment systems will generally use short channels because of the high degree of technical support and liaison needed. Length can also be affected by the size of the manufacturer, its financial capacity, and its desire for control. In general, large and better financed manufacturers have a greater capability to bypass intermediaries and use a shorter chain. Manufacturers desiring to exercise a high degree of control over the distribution of their products use a shorter chain. Retailers do not

It is important to remember that, in many cases, indirect channels are actually cheaper in terms of total costs involved.

SUPPLY CHAIN WIDTH

Supply chain width is usually described in terms of

- Intensive distribution,
- Selective distribution and
- Exclusive distribution.

Intensive distribution means that all possible retailers are used to reach the target market. It is associated with the distribution of convenience goods that are frequently purchased; the consumer is not willing to expend a great deal of effort to purchase.

Selective distribution means that a smaller number of retailers are used, while exclusive distribution means only one retailer is used in the trading area. Selective distribution is associated with shopping goods, items for which the consumer will make a price/value comparison before purchasing.

Exclusive distribution is identified with specialtiy goods – products that the consumer expressly seeks out. Thus, soft drinks, milk, and greeting cards (convenience goods) tend to be carried by a very large umber of retailers; home appliances and apparel (shopping goods) are handled by relatively fewer retailers; and specialtiy goods such as Rolex watches are featured by only one dealer in a trading area.

Exclusive Distribution Selective Distribution Intensive Distribution

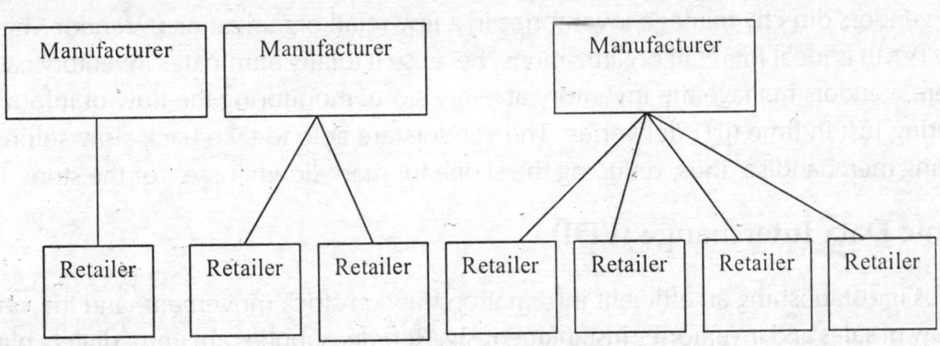

Figure 5

INTEGRATED SUPPLY CHAIN

The end to end integration of all supply chain elements and functions are achieved by applying interlinked packages for perfect information management. The integrated supply chain starts from the design stage at the vendor level to the time when there is consumer response at the retail stage.

The benefits of having an integrated supply chain are

- Achieving the best delivery performance,
- Reduction in inventory,
- Faster fulfillment of cycle time,
- Accuracy in forecasts,
- Lower supply chain costs,
- Improvement in overall productivity and
- Improvement in capacity utilization

VENDOR MANAGEMENT

Efficient vendor management involves selecting the right vendors capable of giving the right quality of merchandise and meeting delivery deadlines. Besides, they should be able to deliver the right quantities as well, so that the retailer can get the right 'hit ratio'. The right hit ratio measures the gap between delivery and purchase orders and helps eliminate backlog in deliveries. In a chain store scenario, vendors directly delivering to stores are an important element in attaining good supply chain efficiency.

The vendors directly manage inventories in a few retail organizations. Vendor Managed Inventory (VMI) is ideal for retail organizations. Because it totally eliminates inventory carrying costs. Here, vendors manage the inventory at every store, monitoring the flow of information and ensuring just in time (JIT) deliveries. The vendors are able to take back slow selling and non-moving merchandise, thus, reducing the scope for mark-down losses for the store

Electronic Data Interchange (EDI)

Helps in establishing an efficient information flow on stock movement, and the vendors get to know of sales and inventories instantaneously. Reorder supplies are immediately planned and executed by the vendors. This process eliminates the time taken to exchange documents for placing orders, thus achieving just in time inventory management. EDI is done through web enabled servers or with the help of the organization's ERP (Enterprise Resource Planning) package that interacts with the vendors' systems.

Warehouse Management

The retail warehouse or the distribution centre (DC) performs the functions of receiving the ordered stocks; checking for the right quality, quantity, and price; temporary storing and docking; tagging the merchandise with both the MRP and security tags; preparing and readying the merchandise; transporting the merchandise; receiving goods returned from retail stores, if any; and sending returned merchandise to vendors back as returns or for refinishing.

Goods Received Note (GRN)

GRN is prepared when the merchandise received at the warehouse from suppliers/ vendors is checked and matched with the relevant purchase order (PO) after certifying all the elements of quality, quantity, etc. The GRN is then automatically recognized by the system after authorization for payment to the vendor by the accounts department. The merchandise is then docked and tagged with bar codes and price tags. If bar coding for MRP has already been done by the vendor, it saves a great deal of time for the retail organization. Then only the security tagging needs to be done at the warehouse.

Inter–Transfer Note (ITN)

This is made when the prepared and readied merchandise is supplied to the retail stores. The reverse ITN is prepared when goods are sent back to the warehouse by the retail store. Goods that are returned to the warehouse are then sent back to the suppliers and vendors. The system recognizes the same and raises a debit note to the vendors.

Transportation

Transportation is done according to timely delivery schedules so that replenishments are delivered as per the plan. Cost efficiency and reduction in delivery time are critical success factors in transportation.

Efficient Docking

Efficient docking with a plan ensures the best utilization of space. Docking ensures that the First in First out (FIFO) delivery plan is followed so that ageing of merchandise in the warehouse is kept to the minimum.

Material Handling Equipment

Material handling equipment in the warehouse should be tailored for specific varieties of merchandise. At a micro level of handling, most of the time garments are delivered by hangers and sometimes by the browser itself in a ready to sell state.

Value Chain

The entire SCM process is a value chain where bottlenecks value adding factors and liability factors are identified and addressed. This enables the retail organization to have an efficient supply chain. The entire process needs to be audited to meet timelines. It may be reengineered to achieve cost efficiencies and reduce cycle times. The supply chain is the heart of retail operations that ensures that the right product is in the right place, at the right time and the right cost.

RETAIL AUTOMATION AND SUPPLY CHAIN MANAGEMENT

The principal objective of introducing supply chain management in a retail organization is to satisfy the customer at the right time with the right product at the right cost, all the time. Integrated systems help bring about efficiencies so that the customer is satisfied every time. The challenges that a retail organization faces are many.

- Huge stock keeping units,
- Seasonal variations of product lines necessitating the introduction of a new Stock Keeping Units,
- Complex tax structures,
- The sheer geographic spread of the country,
- Changing consumer demands, *etc.*

A retail organization has to plan to make this system work perfectly and try to satisfy the needs of every customer without fail. Automation–through the implementation of ERP systems – has helped many organizations improve their efficiency and helped them grow.

The discovery of automatic identification technologies has been a boon to retailing; they were first introduced globally in the 1960s to assist logisticians identify products in the supply chain. The global development of such SCM technologies has been very rapid. There were barcodes, touch memory and multi dimensional barcodes. In India the development of SCM technologies has come a long way. Retailers in the organized sector are beginning to barcode all their products; organizations like Food World and Shoppers' Stop have urged their vendors to supply merchandise only with standard barcodes.

Most retailers in the organized sector in India have to use retail software in their back end and front end operation. They are constantly looking to upgrade their systems as they evolve. To help this growing retail sector get the best, many Indian software companies have developed software packages to suit the different and varied requirements of these retailers. Among the few who are in the market is Chennai based Polaris Retail Infotech ltd, a subsidiary of Polaris, which has entered the market with the software, Retail Excel. Reputed organizations like Wipro Infotech, Tata consultancy services and NCR technologies have created robust retail automation software. The Chennai based TV Sundaram Iyengar and sons are currently test marketing their new point of sale system for small and medium retailers in grocery and other related segments. The list of that developing retail software is growing by the day. There are many other packages like MS Retail, Shopper, Retail Pro, Retail Magik, *etc.*, that help enable the fast implementation of retail automation in India available in the market.

Questions

I. Fill in the Blanks

1. ________ is an end to end process in merchandise planning and movement.
2. ________ are supply chain members that can take title to goods.
3. A ________ occurs when manufacturers sell their goods directly to the final consumers.
4. ________ is ideal for retail organization.
5. ________ with a plan ensures the best utilization of space.

Answers

1. Supply Chain Management 2. Primary marketing institutions
3. direct supply chain 4. Vendor Management Inventory
5. Efficient docking

II. Choose the Best Answer

1. SCM means ______________.
   (a) Stock Control Management (b) Stores Convenient Management
   (c) Supply Chain Management (d) Standard Cost Management
2. __________ institutions take title to the goods.
   (a) Primary marketing (b) Facilitating (c) Financial (d) Commercial
3. Manufacturer sell their goods directly to consumers is ________ supply chain.
   (a) short (b) long (c) direct (d) indirect
4. Expensive, highly technological items use ________ channels.
   (a) short (b) long (c) direct (d) indirect
5. In ________ distribution all possible retailers are used to reach the target market
   (a) intensive (b) selective (c) competitive (d) exclusive

Answers

1. c 2. a 3. c 4.a 5.a

III. Answer in One Sentence

1. What is supply chain management?
2. What do you mean by supply chain length?
3. What is meant by direct supply chain?
4. What do you mean by intensive distribution?
5. What is inter transfer note?

IV. Essay Type Questions

1. Explain the facilitating marketing institutions
2. Discuss the types of supply chain
3. Describe in detail about selective distribution
4. Describe in detail about intensive distribution

Chapter

10

RETAIL PROMOTION STRATEGIES

INTRODUCTION

Retail promotion involves a mix of communication activities carried out by retailers in order to make a positive influence on the customer's perception, attitude and behavior. Retail promotion is broadly defined as all communication that informs, persuades and/or reminds the target market about marketing mix of the retail firm. The basic purpose is to inform customers about retailer, build appealing brand images of their merchandise and the services offered.

Through a promotional campaign, a retailer seeks to

- Provide information and knowledge about the products to the consumers
- Ensure that the consumer develops a favourable attitude towards the retailer and his products and sell their merchandise.

All retailers strive to achieve the most effective response from the target market, *i.e.*, develop a continuous Increase in demand for their product or services. Retailers use promotion to generate sales by making their targeted customers aware, interested and desiring of current offerings. Retailers devote significant sums to promotion. For e.g,, a typical departmental store spends nearly four per cent of sales on ads and eight to ten per cent on personal selling and support services.

ELEMENTS OF RETAIL PROMOTIONAL MIX

Advertising, public relations, personal selling and sales promotion are the elements of promotion. The promotion mix is managed by the retail firm's marketing and advertising department. In some cases, retailers and manufacturers pool in resources for effective promotional strategy.

Retailers employ a combination of advertising, sales promotion, personal selling and publicity to achieve promotional objectives. The degree and nature of usage of each of the promotion methods depends on the objectives of the retail firm, product, market profile and availability of resources. For e.g., Haldiram, the Delhi-Centric food chain, primarily relies on point of purchase materials, neon signs on the restaurant exterior and lately FM radio channels for its promotion.

METHODS OF COMMUNICATING WITH CUSTOMERS

1. Paid impersonal communications
2. Paid personal communications
3. Unpaid impersonal communications
4. Unpaid personal communications

Methods/Forms of Retail Promotion

Particulars	Impersonal	Personal
Paid	Advertising Store atmosphere Visual merchandising Sales promotion Web sites	Personal selling
Unpaid	Publicity	Word of mouth

PAID IMPERSONAL COMMUNICATION METHODS

Paid impersonal communication methods include advertising, stores atmosphere, visual merchandising, sales promotion and web sites.

Advertising

Advertising is paid, non–personal communication transmitted through out of store mass media by an identified sponsor. Four aspects of this definition are:

(i) Paid form

(ii) Non–personal presentation

(iii) Out of store mass media like newspapers, radio, TV and the web and

(iv) Identified sponsor.

Retail advertising's function is primarily to inform potential buyers of the availability and price of a retailer's offering with the objective of developing consumer preferences for a particular retailer.

Objectives of Advertising

A retailer would select one or more of these goals and base advertising efforts on it.

- To lift short term sales
- To increase customer traffic
- To enforce a retail image
- To inform customers about goods and services and/or company attributes
- To ease the job for sales personnel
- To develop demand for private brands
- To reach out to people not accessible to salesmen.
- To manage competition in the market by stimulating sales
- To enhance the goodwill of the retail organization
- To promote new products
- To improve dealer relations

Types of Advertising

The various types of advertising include

- Product advertising
- Mark down event advertising
- Institutional advertising
- Co–operative advertising
- Financial advertising
- Classified advertising
- Informative advertising

Product Advertising

It is used to promote merchandise which is new, exclusive and superior in certain specific aspects of quality, design and its benefits.

Mark–down Event Advertising

This advertising is to create excitement about a particular period during which the products are being offered at lower prices by the retailers.

Institutional Advertising

This type of advertising is used to highlight about the benefits of the shopping centre or shopping mall as a pleasurable place to visit and shop. This types of advertising communicates about the availability of the range of stores, parking facilities *etc.*,

Financial Advertising

It refers to advertisements by various financial institutions like State Bank of India, ICICI *etc.* They provide information about the investment opportunities and the risks and benefits associated with them. HDFC bank evolved a mix of sales promotion and advertising to attract new customers and retain its existing customers.

Classified Advertising

It refers to messages, which are placed under specific headings and columns in various magazines and newspapers, e.g., furniture for sale, situations vacant, *etc.*

Informative Advertising

Purchase of durables products are generally erratic and often too expensive to buy. The buyer requires elaborate information about durable goods. Hence, the retailer and the manufacturer spend a huge amount on informative advertising.

Cooperative Advertising

The costs of retail advertising are shared by manufacturers or wholesalers and their retailers. Two or more retailers may also share costs. Both of these approaches entail cooperative advertising.

Significance of Advertising in the Retail Sector

Advertising is not only the provider of information about products, services and availability at different retail locations, but also an important link in the retail sector between the advertiser and the receiver of the message. Its imperativeness has increased in this era of globalization and liberalization around the world. It has benefits not only for the manufacturers and traders, but for the retailers as well.

Advantages of Advertising

1. A large audience is attracted and circulation is supplemented by the passing of a copy from one reader to another.
2. The costs per reader are low
3. The retailer has control over message content, graphics, training and size.
4. In print media, a message can be studied and restudied by the target market.
5. Self–service or reduced service operations are possible since a customer becomes aware of a retailer and its offerings before shopping.

Benefits of Retail Advertisements to Customers

1. It helps in creating awareness among the customers about the existence, prices and availability of products at different locations.
2. It educates customers about new products and its uses.
3. It ensures the supply of products of better quality.

Disadvantages of Advertising

1. Standardized messages lack flexibility. They do not focus on the needs of individual customers.
2. Some media require large investments. This may reduce the access of small firms.
3. Media may reach large geographic areas, and for retailers, this may be wasteful.
4. Some media require a long lead time for placing ads. This reduces the ability to fad items.
5. Some media have a high throwaway rate. For eg, circulars may be discarded without being read.

Sales Promotion

Sales promotion is another form of paid impersonal communication, which offers additional value and incentive to the customer. Sales promotion is an important controllable variable used by marketing managers. It can create psychological associations in the buyer's mind, with the power to change their purchasing pattern. The most popular sales promotion tools in retailing are premium coupons, in-store displays, contests, product demonstration and sampling, sales promotion tools are excellent demand creators.

There are two strategies in sales promotion. They are pull and push promotion strategies.

Pull Promotion Strategy where consumers are offered various incentives in the form of free samples, discount coupons.

Push Promotion strategy where dealers are offered incentives such as target based incentives, display schemes for dealers and so on.

Objectives of Sales Promotion

Sales promotion efforts are generally designed to assist the other communication activities undertaken by a store. For example, awareness may be generated through advertising but sales promotion may be used tactically to overcome any resistance to purchase. The desire may be created by advertising, but its conversion into sales would be done by sales promotion by offering a short term incentive. Thus, a quicker sales response results from sales promotion. The various objectives of sales promotion can be summed up as follows:

- **Stop and Shop**

Customers, who are just passing by, with no intention of purchasing, would be encouraged to enter the store. The promotional activity may be such that it does not directly hint at a purchase, but just a free trial.

- **Shop and Buy**

Once the customers have been persuaded to enter the store, they have to be convinced to purchase by presenting the merchandise in such a manner that the customer feels a desire to buy.

- **Buy Bigger**

The promotional activity aims to persuade the customers to buy in a greater quantity or buy other products in addition. For example, customers who buy a bigger pack may be entitled to enter into a contest or they can get a free gift or customers who purchase merchandise more than a specified amount would get similar benefits.

- **Repeat Purchase**

The final objective is to encourage customers to come/visit again and again to the store. This is achieved by instilling loyalty among the customers through previous purchases. The goodwill can be created by schemes like continuity programmes or store cards. Regular customers are offered cards whereby after a certain amount of purchases they are entitled to a gift.

Types of Promotion

Retailers break sales promotions into two categories: those where they are the sole sponsors and those involving a joint effort with other parties. These are shown in Figure 1

CATEGORIES OF SALES PROMOTION

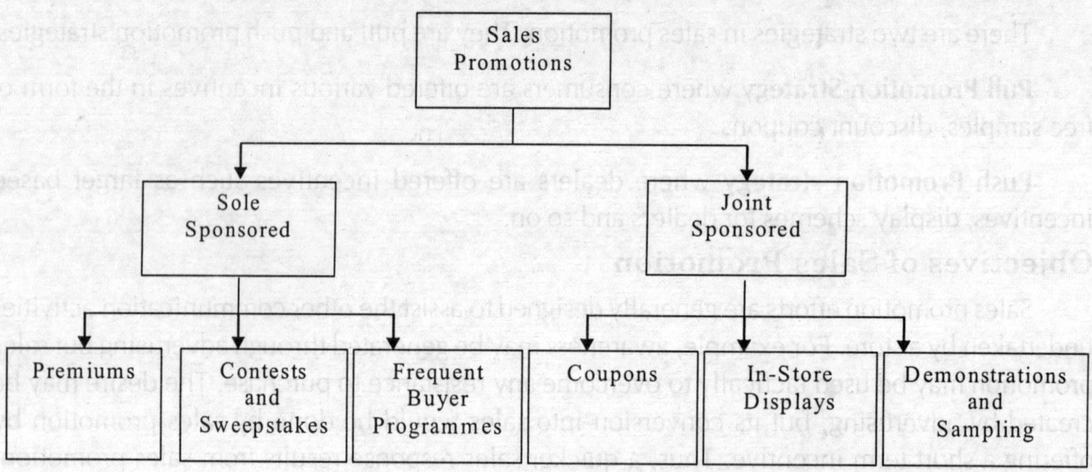

Figure 1

Sole Sponsored Sales Promotion

Sales promotions are an expense to the retailer that may or may not be shared with others. With sole sponsored sales promotions, the retailer has complete control over the promotion, but is also completely responsible for the costs. Retailers generally consider the following promotions to be sole sponsored.

1. **Premiums** are extra items offered to the customer when purchasing a promoted product. Premiums are used to increase consumption among current consumers and persuade

nonusers to try the promoted product. Generally the retailer is solely responsible for such programs.

2. **Contests and Sweepstakes** are designed to create an interest in the retailer's product and encourage both repeat purchases and brand switching. Many local restaurants use weekly drawings not only to generate business, but also to track their customers.
3. **Loyalty Programs** are rapidly growing as retailers realize the importance of combining such promotions with their database system to solidify their relationship with the customer.

Joint Sponsored Sales Promotions

Retailers generally consider the following promotions to be jointly sponsored

1. **Coupons** offer the retail customer a discount on the price of a specific item. For manufacturers, a coupon is a form of advertising to entice a consumer to try a product. Coupons are also used to maintain a loyal base of customers for older brands.
2. **In-store Displays** are promotional displays that seek to generate traffic, advertise, and encourage impulse buying. Displays offer manufacturers a captive audience for their products in the retailer's store. As a result, the manufacturer is willing to pay for the right to "rent" the space necessary for this display from the retailer.
3. **Demonstration and Sampling** are in store presentations or showings whose intent is to reduce the consumer's perceived risk of purchasing a new product.These demonstrations are paid for by the manufacturer at a price that is usually higher than the retailer's cost for providing that service.

Point of Purchase

Most suppliers produce sales aid materials which are placed near the products to attract customers and induce them to purchase. Examples of these types of material are:

- **Leaflets** – These provide details of the product, the advantages of a particular retailer's products over the competitor, unique features and benefits, price, *etc.* For example, leaflets providing information about a particular model of a car are kept in a car showroom.
- **Special Fittings** – The products are kept in the special racks or stands provided by the suppliers. For example, racks provided by toothbrush suppliers, dry – battery stands, glass case for watches, *etc.* These fittings make the product prominent compared to other products kept in normal racks. As these fittings are large and attractive, and kept at conspicuous places, they attract the attention of the customers.
- **Demonstrators** – Sometimes, demonstrators are used in this context. For example, a children's product may use a person dressed as their logo (for example a teddy bear) in the store. Such a person can give away samples of the product. He may stand near the rack storing the product to induce purchases.

Many retailers use the display material provided by suppliers very selectively due to the danger of producing a cluttered and uncoordinated retailing environment. If every supplier wants his individual rack to be placed in the store, it would lead to a much disorganized environment. And since every supplier has his distinct looking stand, the store would lose its consistency in appeal. In some cases, the suppliers and retailers collaborate to produce a mutually acceptable point of sale display material.

STEPS IN DESIGNING RETAIL SALES PROMOTIONS

It is important to evolve a well designed promotion plan to be able to obtain its key benefits. For this purpose, the following steps can be employed by the retailer:

1. Set goals
2. Analyze benefits
3. Design the offer
4. Identify the sources for promotion
5. Design the response and follow up

Set Goals

This should be determined on the basis of the long term goals of the retail organization. It should also be determined by the particular needs of a specific promotion scheme and contextual factors like time of the year – Diwali, Christmas, wedding season, Valentine's day *etc.* The specific promotion policies of the retail organization and the concerned manufacturer should also be kept in mind.

Analyze Benefits

In identifying possible sales promotions, it is important to ensure that everyone involved, including the customer get benefits.

The benefits might be in the form of:

- Access to customer information due to the creation of database of the users of the promotion activity.
- The 'feel good' factor promotion may create both for the customer and the manufacturer
- Reinforcement of the retailer's image
- Provision of rewards to customers
- Stimulation of trial
- Increased sales
- Value addition, special offers, cheaper prices, learning opportunities *etc.* offered to customers, especially loyal shoppers.

Design the Offer

The promotion offer can be designed either economic benefits or experimental benefits or combination of both. Providing a unique experience can involve offers like dinner with a celebrity, free tickets to some sports event or movies, *etc.* These days most of the retailers, particularly in the life style segment, are devising their promotion mix to extend experiential benefits rather than some economic benefits. This helps retailers to communicate with their privileged segment more effectively.

Identify Sources of Sales Promotion

Identifying sources of sales promotion involves evaluating the various media to distribute and display the message.

Designing the Response and Follow-up

Sometimes the promotional tools do not realize their full potential because the response mechanism is too complicated or unclear. It should be easy to respond by ticking a box, picking up the phone, handing over the coupon, and so on. There is a risk in giving people too many choices, as it can take too long to work out what to do. On the other hand, customers like offers to be as flexible as possible. When the retailer designs a response plan for sales promotion, the prime consideration is: Is it easy for the customer?

Other key things to remember are:

- How will the target customer for the offer be identified?
- Would it be possible to keep the customer's name and address for the future?
- Is the sales promotion method foolproof and will it reflect well on the retail organization?
- Can the logistics of the programme be easily managed?

Advantages of Sales Promotion

The key advantages of retail sales promotions relate to its eye catching appeal and distinctive value offer associated with it. Its advantages are listed below:

- It has often eye catching appeal
- Themes and tools can be distinctive
- The consumer may receive something of value such as coupons of free merchandising
- Impulse purchases are increased
- It helps to draw customer traffic and maintain loyalty to the retailer.

Disadvantages of Sales Promotion

The major disadvantages of sales promotion are:

- It may be difficult to terminate certain promotions without adverse customer reactions
- The retailer's image may be hurt if corny promotions are used
- Sometimes frivolous selling points are stressed rather than retailers' product assortment, prices, customer services, and other factors.
- Many sales promotions have only short term effects

Store Atmosphere

The in-store environment like layout, signs and displays colors and lighting effects, pleasing music and visual merchandising can have a positive influence in drawing customers to the stores. They can create the right appeal and image of the store in the customers' mind. Stores loyalty can be created by pleasant service, suitable pricing and attractive display of its merchandise.

Retailers' Website

Most of the leading retailers have created their own websites to communicate with their customers. The websites are used by retailers to build their brand image, inform customers about their merchandise, location of the store, attractive pricing of their merchandise, special schemes and events and also to sell their merchandise online.

Visual Merchandising

Visual merchandising is defined as the presentation of products in order to sell them. The initial point of interaction with a potential customer is in the window displays of the storefront. When a retailer arranged his goods to be more attractive to a customer, or when a farmer put the best of his harvest on the top of the basket for the consumers to see and touch, that was visual merchandising.

PAID PERSONAL COMMUNICATIONS INCLUDE PERSONAL SELLING

Personal Selling

It involves oral communication with one or more prospective customers for the purpose of marketing and sales. Personal selling is a form of communication process where the retail sales–persons through a face to face interaction with customers trying to satisfy their needs. The level of personal selling used by a retailer depends on the image it wants to convey, the products sold, the amount of self service, and the interest in long–term customer relationships as well as customer expectations. Retail sales–people may work in a store, visit consumer homes or places of work or engage in tele–marketing.

Objectives of Personal Selling

The goals of personal selling are to

1. Persuade customers to buy
2. Stimulate sales of impulse items or products related to customers' basic purchases
3. Complete customer transactions
4. Feed back information to company decision makers
5. Provide proper levels of customer service
6. Improve and maintain customer satisfaction
7. create awareness of items marketed through the web, mail, and telemarketing

The objectives of personal selling can be demand oriented and/or image oriented. The former focuses on pushing sales for the product, while the latter attempts to build the store image. Demand oriented objectives relate to providing information, persuading the customer, and reminding him about the products, services and the related experience. Image oriented objectives relate to building the retail knowledge and generating the trust among customers and the larger community.

Types of Personal Selling

Most sales positions involve either order taking or order getting. An order taking sales–person performs routine clerical and sales functions – setting up displays, stocking shelves, answering simple questions and ringing up sales. This type of selling is most likely in stores that are strong in self service but also have some personnel on the floor. An order getting salesperson is actively involved with informing and persuading customers, and in closing sales. This is true of "sales" employee. Order getters usually sell higher priced or complex items, such as real estate, autos and consumer electronics. They are more skilled and better paid than order takers.

A manufacturer may sometimes help personal selling by providing promotional or push monies (PMS) for retail salespeople selling its brand. PMS are in addition to regular salesperson compensation. Many retailers dislike this practice because their salespeople may be less responsive to actual customer desires.

Advantages of Personal Selling

The advantages of selling relate to its personal nature:

(1) A salesperson adopt a message to the needs of the individual customer

(2) A salesperson can be flexible in offering ways to address customer needs

(3) The attention span of the customer is higher than with advertising

(4) There is less waste; most people who walk into a store are potential customers

(5) Customers respond more often to personal selling than to ads.

(6) Immediate feedback is provided.

Disadvantages of Personal Selling

The major disadvantages of personal selling are:

(1) Only a limited number of customers can be handled at a given time.

(2) The costs of interacting with each customer can be high.

(3) Customers are not initially lured into a store through personal selling

(4) Self–service may be discouraged

(5) Some customers may view sales–people as unhelpful and as too aggressive

UNPAID IMPERSONAL COMMUNICATIONS

Publicity and public relations are two forms of unpaid impersonal communications.

Publicity is a non–personal form of promotion where messages are transmitted through mass media, the time or space provided by media is not provided for and there is no identified commercial sponsor. The basic distinction between advertising and publicity is that publicity is non–paid. As a result, publicity is not as readily controllable. Publicity is more credible and valuable than ads. Advertising and publicity should complement each other. Many times, publicity should precede advertising,

Public Relations entail any communication that fosters a favorable image for the retailer among its public (consumers, investors, government, channel members, employees, and the general public). It may be non–personal or personal, paid or non–paid, and sponsor controlled or not controlled. Public relations can benefit both large and small retailers. While the former often spend a lot of money to publicize events, small firms can creatively generate attention for themselves on a limited budget.

Objectives of Public Relations

Public relations seek to accomplish one or more of these goals:

- Increase awareness of the retailer and its strategy mix.
- Maintain or improve the company image.
- Show the retailer as a contributor to the public's quality of life
- Demonstrate innovativeness
- Present a favorable message in a highly believable manner
- Minimize total promotion costs

Advantages of Public Relations

The major advantages of public relations are that:

- An image can be presented or enhanced
- A more credible source presents the message (such as a good restaurant review)
- There are no costs for the message's time or space
- A mass audience is addressed
- Carryover effect are possible (if a store is perceived as community oriented, its value positioning is more apt to be perceived favorably)
- People pay more attention to news/stories than to clearly identified ads

Disadvantages of Public Relations

The major disadvantages of public relations are that:

- Some retailers do not believe in spending in funds on image related communication
- There is little retailer control over a publicity message and its timing, placement, and coverage by a given medium.
- It may be more suitable for short run, rather than long run planning
- Although there are no media costs for publicity, there are costs for a public relations staff, planning activities, and the activities themselves (such as store openings)

UNPAID PERSONAL COMMUNICATIONS

The word of mouth communication between the customers and the retailer is personalized and involves no additional cost to the latter. When satisfied customers become opinion leaders and convey a positive picture of the retailer and his merchandise to their friends and colleagues, it will help to create a positive impression on the store's performance. At the same time, retailers also need to exercise care and provide good merchandise and serve their customers properly, or else unfavorable word of mouth can adversely affect the store's performance.

SELECTION OF PROMOTIONAL MIX

While deciding on the use of the communication methods, the retailer will have to make a comparison in terms of control, flexibility, credibility and cost.

Control

Retailers will have more control when using paid against unpaid communication method. While using paid communications media such as advertising, sales promotion, store atmospherics, websites, email, the retailers can have control over the time of its delivery. However, retailers cannot have control over the delivery of each salesperson's performance or

COMPARISON OF VARIOUS RETAIL PROMOTION METHODS

Media	Advantages	Limitations	Examples
Newspapers	Flexibility, timeliness, good local market coverage, broad acceptance, high believability	Short life, poor reproduction quality, small 'pass–along' audience	The Hindustan Times, The Times of India, The Indian Express.
Television	Combines sight, sound and notion, appealing to the senses, high attention, high reach.	High cost and clutter, fleeting exposure, less audience selectivity.	Zee TV, Sony Star TV, DD Metro
Direct Mail	Audience selectivity, flexibility no ad competition within the same medium, personalization	Relatively high cost, 'junk mail' image	E-mail/ letter/ fax
Radio	Mass use, high demographic and geographic selectivity, credibility and prestige, high quality reproduction, long life, good 'pass along'	Audio presentation, lower attention than television, non standardized rate structures, high exposures	Radio 98.3 FM, Vividh Bharti
Magazines	High geographic and demographic selectivity, credibility and prestige, high quality reproduction, long life. Good 'pass along' readership.	Long ad purchases lead time, waste circulation, no guarantee of position.	Business World, Femina, India Today, Cosmopolitan

Outdoor	Flexible, high repeat exposure, low cost, low competition	Limited audience selectivity, creative limitations.	Hoardings posters, banners, neon signs, balloons.
Yellow pages	Excellent local coverage, high believability, wide	High competition, long ad purchase lead time, creative limitations.	Tata Press Yellow pages
Newsletters	High selectivity, full control, interactive opportunities	High cost	Mall times by Ansal Plaza, New Delhi.
Brochures	Flexibility, full control, can dramatize messages	Over production leads to run away costs	Be:, John Player
Telephone	Many users, to opportunity give a	High cost unless volunteers are used	Just Dial services, MTNL
Word of mouth	No cost, from consumers , for consumers, by consumers, enhances reputation	No control, decides its own course (positive or negative); needs hard to counteract the negative	Local retailers, professional services (medical, financial analysis)
Flyers	Inexpensive, easy to administer, no frills required, use pictures, easy to change, wide	Mistaken for junk, limited life, limited information can be communicated	Small retailers, restaurants
Vehicle signs	One time cost, visible 24*7, find place on business and personal vehicles, use words or pictures	Limited space to display, owner may object, durability is limited.	Car showrooms, accessories stores, auto services.
Internet	High selectivity, interactive possibilities, relative low cost	New media with a low number of users in some countries	Yahoo, Rediff, India times.

even over the content and timing of publicity and word of mouth communications. Further, in case of unpaid communication media, since it is designed and delivered by persons not employed by the retailers, they can communicate either favorable or unfavorable information.

Flexibility

Personal selling, emails and websites can be personalized and used by the retailers depending upon the customer's specific needs and requirements. But the other methods such as advertising, sales promotion, *etc.*, are mass communication methods and it will be difficult to personalize them.

Credibility

Customers will usually find publicity and word of mouth communication to be more creditable sources of information since they are independent persons like friends and family who are personally known to them. Whereas, when salespersons and advertising are used by retailers, the customers may not fully believe the claims made by them because they think that these are methods used to promote the retailer's merchandise.

Cost

Publicity and word of mouth communication involve expenses to the extent that retailers have to incur costs to stimulate them. Advertising is reasonably economical because it addresses the mass audience at the same time. Whereas, personal selling involves more cost because salary has to be paid to the retail sales persons on a continuous basis. Emails can be sent to customers at low cost. However, it may be costly to design, update continuously and promote the site to attract visitors although maintaining a website may be relatively inexpensive

MEDIA SELECTION

The retailers usually make a choice from alternative media categories by taking into account factors like target audience, media habits, product profile, message compatibility and cost. Retailers need to review periodically the impact and cost of various media types available. In the recent past, Indian retailers started using different media channels. Earlier, a good number of media channels like TV and radio used to serve a limited purpose for the retailer making their use generally unattractive.

The most popular and readily available media is the store itself which effectively employs store atmospherics to powerfully convey the desired image and message. Along with the usage of promotional vehicles such as price tags, displays, packaging material, supermarkets sell the space on their floors for company logos, occasionally experimenting with shelves and introduction of 'video carts'. Even in the best selling paper books, theatres, and movie videotapes, the written material which consists of annual reports, data sheets, and catalogues increasingly carry advertisements. Many companies even mail audio/video tapes of their products to prospective customers. Many large and small retailers use sponsorships to communicate their message and also obtain the desired publicity.

Media selection involves finding the most cost effective media to deliver the desired number of exposures to the target audience. In the desired number of exposures the advertiser seeks a certain response from target audience, *e.g.*, a certain level of product trial and the level of brand awareness among the audience. The effect of exposures on audience depends on reach, frequency, and impact.

- **Reach (R):** It includes the different persons or households that are exposed to a particular media schedule at least once during a specified time period.
- **Frequency (F):** The number of times within the specified time period that an average person or household is exposed to the message.
- **Impact (I):** The qualitative value of an exposure through a given medium.

The relationship between reach, frequency, and impact is captured through the following concepts:

- **Total Number of Exposures (E):** It is the reach times the average frequency, *i.e.*, E = RxF . This measure is referred to as gross rating points (GRP)
- **Weighted Number of Exposures (WE):** It is the reach times frequency times average impact, *i.e.*, WE = R + F+ I

The media planner has to figure out, with a given budget, the most cost effective combination of reach, frequency, and impact. Reach is most important for launch purchased products, flanker brands, extensions of well known brands or infrequently purchased brands, or going after undefined target market. Frequency is most important where there are strong competitors, a complex story to tell, high consumer resistance, or frequency purchase cycle.

POPULAR MEDIA VEHICLES USED IN THE INDIAN RETAIL SECTOR

There is a whole range of vehicles for promotions available to the retailers to choose from. While selecting a particular set of materials for the publicity, retailers have to consider factors such as cost of the selected material, compatibility with their objective, and the rest of the communications strategy. Most Indian retailers rely on vehicles like leaflets, posters, banners, wall paintings, magazines, flyers, direct mails, *etc.* Television is primarily used by retail chains in the organized sector. They largely have a standardized offering across outlets and hence, find it cost effective to approach a wide audience through television advertising. The popular media vehicles are discussed below.

Leaflets or Flyers

Retailers to promote specific activities and events use leaflets or flyers. They have a short shelf life, so they are most useful for marketing specific activities such as opening of a new outlet or off season sale rather than conveying information. The retailers want customers to retain for a long time. Leaflets are inserted into other publications such as newspapers and magazines. The effectiveness of leaflets for a desired objective has to be ensured before using them. Retailers have to give due weightage to the designing of the message.

Posters/Calendars

Retailers use posters to promote specific activities and events, or as free gift to other channel members, especially their loyal customers. This is a very common practice among small retailers in India associated with the festive season of Diwali or New year. Recently even the most established retail chains such as banks and other professional houses opted for it. Retailers need to include contact details on posters and calendars.

Booklets

Retailers from the organized sector can afford this costly mode of communication. It is effective in case of products or services which are intense on information, such as banking, real estate practitioners, fashion designers, and insurance services. Most of the retailers selling consumer durables depend for such support on respective manufacturers rather than investing themselves. The retailers should avoid the temptation to cram too much information into a booklet to lower the production values. This often results in the booklet being difficult to read and can portray a negative image.

Direct Mail

Retailers can opt to send out regular, targeted letters as part of their communication strategy. Direct mail advertising includes postcards, catalogues, brochures, email, and single letters. This technique is considered to be effective at the time of introducing new products and informing about prospective sales and or special discounts. Direct mail advertising is recommended for email firms with a wide selection of merchandise like furniture, music, insurance, clothes, etc. It is a great way to keep current customers aware of new products, services, or sales. It can also be used as a promotional tool for new customers.

This is relatively cost effective way of reaching audiences and one can achieve a much more direct tone of voice. Direct mail letters should be personalized and should be short and to the point, with strong opening and concluding paragraphs. Leading retailers such as Shopper's Shop and other retail chains in the organized sector use this medium to communicate about new arrivals, seasonal discounts, and previews sales.

Magazines

Magazines are considered to be an effective medium to advertise to the target segment. For example, a retailer selling baby products could put an ad in Parenting or Health and Nutrition. Due to the large reach of magazines, this type of advertising is effective for a large retailing chain with a wide customer base. Local and regional magazines also play a crucial role in respect of the small retailers in townships.

Local Cable Channels

With the advent of the local cable TV channels, most of the small retailers use this medium to communicate about their offerings and promotions to their target segment more effectively. Most of the retailers realize cable network is comparatively less costly in comparison to newspapers. It proves to be more effective as most of the family members can be covered through this media. It serves well to launch a new retail outlet, new product range, and above all any promotion or discount information in the catchments area. The retailers can avail of great degree of flexibility of the medium by making changes in the message as need arises or according to the feedback received.

Billboards

It is one of the most famous and convenient media used by retailers in urban areas to communicate their offerings to the people in their catchment area. Most of the leading retailers of the city place their billboards at railway stations or bus stands and at the entrance of the city by road.

They are available in various sizes and give an idea about the structure of the store in the city. Billboard advertising is also a great way to direct people to a store or shopping centre. Retailers to place their billboards, have to pay some local taxes to the local government bodies or private owners. Billboards are an effective medium of advertising for restaurants, hotels, car rental companies, shopping centers, adventure parks, and any types of business that deals with travelling customers.

Wall Paintings

This is the most traditional media used by the small retailers in the villages and townships in India. As it includes cost of paint and the low fee charged by painters, retailers usually get the walls of deserted buildings painted at the outskirts of the city with the name of the store and address. This mode is commonly used even by the leading marketers. Wall painting is a durable form of media with limited degree of flexibility to change the content of the communication.

Banners

Retailers use banners regularly for immediate benefits, such as to make the customers aware about the new arrivals, promotional schemes, or launch of the new store. Banners are messages displayed on cloth, plastic, or hard board. Banners can be wall mounted or ceiling mounted both indoors and outdoors. The cost involved is limited but it provides ample mobility to the retailers to display their banners.

Questions

I. Fill in the Blanks

1. __________ involves a mix of communication activities to make a positive influence on customer attitude.
2. All retailers strive to achieve the most effective response from their __________.
3. __________ is paid personal form of retail promotion.
4. __________ is the attractive presentation of products for sale.
5. Any communication that fosters a favourable image of the retailer among its public is __________.
6. Retailers use __________ to make the customers aware about promotional schemes and new arrivals.

Answers

1. Retail promotion 2. target market 3. Personal selling
4. Visual merchandising 5. public relation 6. banners

II. Choose the Best Answer

1. Advertising, Public relations, personal selling and sales promotion are the elements of __________.
   (a) retailing (b) promotion (c) marketing mix (d) marketing
2. __________ is a personal methods of Retail Promotion.
   (a) Advertising (b) Store atmosphere
   (c) Visual merchandising (d) Personal selling
3. __________ is a paid forms of Impersonal Retail Promotion.
   (a) Advertising (b) Personal selling (c) Publicity (d) Sampling
4. __________ advertising is used to highlight about the benefits of the shopping centre.
   (a) Product (b) Market down event (c) Institutional (d) Informative

5. ________ are extra items offered to the customer when purchasing a promoted product.

   (a) Contest and sweepstakes (b) Loyalty programs

   (c) Premiums (d) Sampling

Answers

1. b 2.d 3.a 4.c 5.c

III. Answer in One Word

1. What are the elements of Retail Promotional Mix?
2. Mention the methods of paid forms of Impersonal Retail Promotion.
3. What is Mark-down event advertising?
4. What is meant by Push Promotion Strategy?
5. What is Point of Purchase?

IV. Essay Questions

1. Explain in detail various methods of retail promotion.
2. Describe in detail various types of advertising.
3. Discuss the significance of advertising in the retail sector.
4. Describe in detail various objectives of sales promotion.
5. Explain in detail various steps in designing retail sales promotion.

Chapter 11

CASE STUDY

VIVEKS LIMITED

Viveks Limited is a professionally managed public Limited company carrying three retail brands –Viveks, Jainsons, and Premier Electronics adding to the formidable strength of 1000 employees. Viveks Ltd is one of the most leading and respected consumer electronics and home appliances retail chain in India. Viveks popularized several brands by creating visibility and has the distinction of being a market leader and trendsetter with continuous support from the principal companies. Reliable services are ensured through cordial customer relationships. CII and Mickinsey raved about the Viveks brand as "more trusted than the brands it sells".

The Story of Viveks

B.A Lakshmi Narayana Setty influenced by the ideals of Swami Vivekananda set up a small shop of 200 sq.ft., at Mylapore Chennai, with an investment of only Rs.10,000 to sell electrical fitting and folding chairs. Added slowly radios, fans, mixers, irons, heaters and other household equipments he named his business Viveks & Co inspired by his Guru Swami Vivekananda. B.A Kodandaraman took over his reins of Viveks after the demise of his brother B.A Lakshmi Narayana Shetty and increased the turnover of Rs. 1.65 lakhs in the first year to a stunning figure of 28 crores by 1980. During the initial stages, the consumer durable electronics were considered as luxury. To make them reach the mass middle class families, Viveks started an in-house easy monthly installments scheme. This helped the company to increase its business and gain new customers.

The Founder had a vision of

- Offering the best products to people on the most affordable terms;
- Rendering uncompromising customer care
- Offering employment to the deserving and the needy
- Serving the larger interests of the Society in ways dear to him

With the opening of two new showrooms at Purusaiwalkam (1968) and T. Nagar (1980), Viveks and Co., broke new ground by being the first to the widest range of consumer durables under one roof. Viveks had spent several years laying the foundation for an explosive growth. Its mission was to be India's first truly **world class, consumer durable retailing chain.** It aimed to achieve this through

- Geographical expansion,
- Upgrading operational standards,
- Widening its product range,
- Offering easy finance solutions and
- Quality advertising, publicity and promotional efforts,
- creating consumer awareness

Its strategy was to offer customers "more" of everything, *viz* More space More products, More brands and models, More service, More attractive promotions. Thus, was born the concept of Viveks "The Unlimited Shop".

While the first 30 years saw the setting up only 3 showrooms, the subsequent 4 years saw spurt of growth – an addition of 50 more showrooms through the expansions and acquisitions. By these strategic initiative for rapid expansion, by incorporating Viveks Ltd. in 1994, established its dominance in the two states on Tamil Nadu and Karnataka with 51 showrooms covering a retail space over 1,75,000 sq.ft and boasting of a group turnover of ₹ 400 crore. The future plans envisage setting up of 50 more showrooms in south India.

Such a meteoric growth has been made possible by the dedicated efforts of the Three Shetty brothers, B.A. Kodandaraman, B. A. Chandrashekar and B.A. Srinivasa who always ensured that Viveks was ahead of its time by creating and establishing competitive, advanced Introducing systems to enhance operational effectiveness, changing with times, without in anyway diluting their CORE BELIEFS of offering the best products to the people on the most affordable terms, passion for the very best products and service, and commitment to quality. Their line of product dealing includes

- Home appliances like Air conditioner, Air cooler, Washing machine, Vacuum cleaner, Water heater, Fan, Refrigerator, Freezer, Dryers, *etc.*
- Consumer Electronics like Audio system, Television, Stabilizer, Invertors, Emergency lamp, Irons, Personal care products *etc.*
- Kitchen Appliances like Food processor, Chopper, Juicer, Toaster, Coffee maker, Gas stove, Electric rice cooker, Wet grinder, Mixer, Microwave ovens, Dishwashers etc.
- Digital products like Cameras, Computers, Mobile phones, Printers, Scanners, UPS, *etc.*

Viveks Agencies

Viveks with a novel approach to retail business, ventured into a new area in the distribution channel. Viveks group realized the importance of an integrated approach to retailing well ahead of time and set up a distribution firm Viveks Agencies in 1976. Starting with the distribution of Sumeet Mixers, the company has added a whole range of products to its distribution basket.

Viveks Service Centre

At Viveks, all initiative is taken towards continuous advancements in serving the customer. One of their recent endeavors is the Viveks Service Centre, set-up to provide comprehensive technical assistance in product services, installations and repair. Viveks Service Centre was inaugurated on 10th September 2004. The Viveks Service Centre incorporates the latest in design and style elements, so as to create a pleasing environment for customers and employees alike. Much attention was paid to create the state of art work conditions for employees and the perfect ambiance for customers. In fact, each customer is received personally and their product is taken in for repairs only after a thorough understanding of its technical problems. The Service Centres operate under a centralized support office which covers all functions of administration, finance, marketing, human resources, inventory and most importantly a good customer support team and a dedicated multi-line customer service call centre. Viveks Service Centre is already the most sought after in service of Sumeet mixers and is fast gaining popularity with other categories. A living testament is the 1,00,000+ customers serviced during the last financial year alone. The Service Centre is authorized by Sumeet, Panasonic, Philips, Kenstar, Samsung, Voltas, Haier, Hitachi, LG, Morphy Richards, and many more. Viveks Service Centre strives to provide a one-stop solution to serve all categories and brands of household consumer durables. Viveks Service Centre is by far the largest consumer durable retailer developed initiative in the country. The flagship outlet is located in the heart of the Chennai city at Mylapore and spreads across 1,00,00 sq.ft., with an additional nine branches located at prominent locations across Chennai. Viveks Service Centre has its own in-house multi-line dedicated Help Desk with trained and courteous manpower assisting customers during every stage of the service. Viveks Service Centre works in collaboration with key manufacturers, enabling a professional approach to servicing with genuine spares, accessories and trained manpower

Awards and Recognitions

- The latest, of national and global importance are.....
- Platinum Award from Panasonic (Ideas for Life) for 2008-2009.
- Usha Fans – Star Performer Modern Retail 2007 -2008.
- Excellence Award from Sowbaghya 2007-2008.
- Highest performance award (chain stores)from Voltas 2007.
- Best Performance award from Sony 2007.

- Star award from Godrej 2006-2007.
- Best dealer award (all categories sales) from Sony 2006.

Images Retail Awards, the first of it's kind in India, held in New Delhi during September 2004 saw Vivek bagging the Retailer of the year Award in the **Consumer Electronics section.**

Vivek also figures in the first ever listing of the top five hundred retailers in the ASIA PACIFIC REGION across all segments of retailing. Needless to add no other retailer of consumer durables in India found a mention in that list!

APOLLO PHARMACY

Apollo Pharmacy is a part of Apollo Hospitals - Asia's largest healthcare group. Apollo Hospitals Group with over 7,500 beds in 35 hospitals, a string of nursing and hospital management colleges, and dual lifeline services, *viz.*, pharmacies and diagnostic clinics, Apollo provides a network of healthcare assurance across Asia.

The first Apollo pharmacy opened in Chennai in 1983. Since then, they have served over one crore customers through their pharmacy chain. Their retailing experience, customer-focused service and brand values make them the preferred partner for customers medicine needs. Apollo pharmacy provide a wide range of pharmacy, surgical, disposables, anti-cancer, life saving and general healthcare products and nutritional supplements. Their priority is to stock an entire range of pharmaceutical and medical products, and delivering them efficiently to their customers. Their back up facility helps them to serve their customers with critical medicines. The vast pharmacy network enables them to provide medicine support to their customers even when they are on move for their treatments.

Figure 1

Figure 2

Apollo Pharmacy is the largest retail pharmacy chain in India. They have over 890 Plus outlets across India, in 20 states including Andaman and Nicobar Islands. Apollo pharmacy customers include a large number of individual consumers besides leading hospitals and clinics, corporate houses and Government bodies across the country. Apollo Pharmacy, a division of Apollo Hospitals Enterprises Ltd., is India's first and largest branded pharmacy network.

Accredited with - International Quality Certification, Apollo Pharmacy offers genuine medicines round-the-clock, through their 24-hour Pharmacies. figure 1 clearly shows 24 hours Apollo Pharmacy. Apollo Pharmacy also provides Customer Care any time of the day. Their 24-hour pharmacy chain offers a variety of retail formats to suit customer requirements. Apollo Pharmacy has transformed the concept of a Medical Shop, into a professionally structured and managed organization. Quality Service to customers is their prime focus, and this is done through Human Resources. The work environment at Apollo Pharmacy is open and informal. People are free to be innovative with ideas that benefit the organization and customers. Ongoing training enables new leadership skills to conquer newer challenges. Team members create a unique pride of ownership among themselves, which is how the organisation has rapidly grown. figure 2 shows team members of Apollo chain. At Apollo Pharmacy, attitude towards one's job is as important as qualifications. Hence, people with the right attitude are constantly moved up to higher positions. Apollo Pharmacy attracts the best talent from various fields. Apollo Pharmacy continuously works towards providing best of their services through its ever increasing network of Apollo Pharmacies and customer care services. Quality is the cornerstone of their existence. They have gained experience in pharmacy operations management over the last 2 decades and are committed to delivering best service in the industry. At Apollo Pharmacy, they believe in adhering to the highest quality standards, while serving consumers. Apollo Pharmacy has tied up with ITC e-choupals (Choupal Sagar) and Godrej Aadhaar to provide quality medicines to rural India. Apollo Pharmacies also cater to the needs of consumers residing overseas

Highlights of Apollo Pharmacy

- The largest pharmacy chain - over 300 outlets across India, open 24 hours.
- Genuine medicines from leading manufacturers.
- Wide range of pharmacy, surgical and disposables, anti-cancer, life saving and general healthcare products.
- Innovation in Pharmacy services like personalised pharmacy-refilling services.
- Comply with the rules described by Drugs and Cosmetics Act of 1948.
- Outlets manned by qualified and trained pharmacist.
- The controlled temperature helps in maintaining quality of medicines and their efficiency on consumption.
- For patients who consume medicines on regular basis they provide prescription refilling service on request.
- Computerised billing discloses the expiry date and batch numbers of medicines.
- The entire supply chain mechanism is computerized; hence redundancies are managed effectively. The system also discloses expiry date and batch numbers for medicines.

VISION

With the most Innovative Retail Management Programs, Services and Technology,

- Serving customers with a better experience in the world of pharmacy, defined by quality, service, value and commitment.
- Providing a suitable ambience to their associates (in the medical fraternity, pharmacy business and those looking out for good health) where they can exhibit their potential and grow favorably.
- Becoming a leading corporate citizen by keeping all the Corporate Social Responsibilities (CSR) in mind and in turn serving the community better.
- Conducting relationship management programs with complete integrity and openness.
- Ensuring a long-term viability with profitability and high market share and thus, maintaining a strong growth phase consistently.

MISSION

To be a Responsive Round-the-clock Pharmacy Retailer to Prospective Customers

Today Apollo Pharmacy is well equipped to provide round-the-clock drug service in India, with the enviable experience of Apollo Group of Hospitals. Their mission also includes offering the easiest, fastest and the most reliable drug store service to their customers in India. They constantly strive hard to facilitate good relationships between the patient, doctor and pharmacist. While meeting the healthcare needs of their customers, they are always in a look out to provide outstanding services and add value by making their purchases as convenient as possible.

Apollo Pharmacy is driven by the disciplines of responsiveness, trust and integrity to serve a diverse group of clientele through their outlets. Their core values are integrity, teamwork, commitment and openness to new ideas. They lay a lot of emphasis on healthy life and concern for customer's health is their prime motive.

TANISHQ AND TITAN

The Tata Group is one of India's oldest, largest and most respected business conglomerates. The Tata Group comprises 96 operating companies in seven business sectors: information systems and communications; engineering; materials; services; energy; consumer products; and chemicals. The Group was founded by Jamsetji Tata in the mid 19th century, a period when India had just set out on the road to gaining independence from British rule. Consequently, Jamsetji Tata and those who followed him aligned business opportunities with the objective of nation building. This approach remains enshrined in the Group's ethos to this day.

Tanishq is India's largest, most desirable and fastest growing jewellery brand in India. Started in 1995, Tanishq is the jewellery business group of Titan Industries Ltd - promoted by the TATA group, India's most respected and widely diversified business conglomerate. Tanishq introduced professional retailing in the dis-organised Indian jewellery bazaar, where women can shop with comfort and peace, without worrying about the purity of the jewellery they are buying, as well as, select from the best jewellery collections available in the Indian market. Tanishq today is India's most aspirational fine jewellery brand with 91 stores in 64 cities, with an exquisite range of gold jewellery studded with diamonds or coloured gems and a wide range of equally spectacular jewellery in 22 Kt pure gold. Exquisite platinum jewellery is also part of the product range. It is a story of a successful Indian enterprise, which has delivered value to its customers and shareholders in a complex category, marked by its completely localized front end as well as back end.

Tanishq has set up production and sourcing bases with through research of the jewellery crafts of India. jewellery at Tanishq is crafted in one of the world's most modern factories. The factory complies with all labour and environmental standards. Located at Hosur, Tamil Nadu, the 1,35,000 sq. ft. factory is equipped with the latest and most modern machinery and equipment. Every product at Tanishq is painstakingly crafted to perfection. Diligent care and quality processes ensure that the Tanishq finish is unmatched by any other jeweller in the country. Tanishq challenged the age-old jeweller's world with TATA's guaranteed purity. It exploded the market with facts about rampant impurity across India. It introduced technology-backed challenge in a category completely governed by individual trust. Tanishq introduced innovations like Karatmeter, the only non–destructive means to check the purity of gold.

The Tanishq jewellery Division has over 70 boutiques in over 50 cities across the length and breadth of India. At Tanishq it's not just the products, it's the experience that matters. It ensure the premium quality of not only product but service as well. Tanishq not only has an exquisite range of designs to meet all customer requirements but also offer the benefit of any modification or customization on products. There are host of value added services that one can avail of at Tanishq like the Golden Harvest Savings Scheme, Gift Voucher purchase, Exchange of gold and diamonds, etc.

Tanishq the "Revitaliser of Tradition"

Tanishq has opened first-of-its-kind concept stores at Kolkata, South Extension Delhi, Kormangala Bangaluru and Bund Garden, Pune. These stores reflect the new retail identity of Tanishq the 'Revitaliser of Tradition' and combine the grandeur of the past with the reality of the present without losing its inherent character and appeal.

The introduction of the idea of a concept store catapults Tanishq's unique brand identity in the retail space and takes jewellery retailing in India to a new level. The concept stores will take Tanishq closer to making it the complete jewellery brand catering to varying consumer needs and tastes across all consumer segments and also provide customers a unique and innovative buying experience.

The theme 'Revitalizer of Tradition' has been incorporated in all the design aspects for the new concept stores. The stores have a contemporary feel while retaining the flavor of the past. Traditional craftsmen were used to create a period ambience so that the store replicates the authentic period look with its stunning sand stone arches and special motifs inspired by the inlay work of the Taj Mahal for the North and East stores and the Chettinad influences for the South stores. Tanishq has plans to extend its retail experience to a larger consumer base by launching more concept stores across the country. Tanishq jewellery is exported to Europe, U.S.A., Middle East and Australia.

TITAN

The significance of the name TITAN connotes the association of the Tata Group in the form of Tata Industries and the Tamil Nadu Industrial Development Corporation. It thus signifies the joint venture between the Tata Group and TIDCO. The Manufacturers of India's leading watch brand and India's only national jewellery brand - using design, technology and people for unchallenged market leadership. The Joint Venture between India's most respected business organization - the Tata Group and the Tamil Nadu Industrial Development Corporation (TIDCO) is, World's sixth largest manufacturer of watches and India's leading producer of watches under the Titan and Sonata brand names. Product portfolio includes watches, jewellery, eyewear and precision engineered products. It exports watches to about 40 countries around the world with manufacturing facilities in Hosur, Dehradun, Goa and manufactures precious jewellery under the Tanishq brand name, making it India's only national jewellery brand.With extensive domestic distribution network, amongst the **world's largest retail chain of exclusive retail showrooms called 'The World of Titan'** with 164 showrooms and multibrand outlets named Time Zones with 144 outlets for watches, Titan watches crossed 70 million customers.

